Disposable Thoughts

Disposable Thoughts

Essays on Reading, Writing, and Relationships

RANDY RUDDER

ISBN-13: 9781453735817
ISBN-10: 145373581X

Dedication:

To my wonderful wife, Clare Rudder, and my precious daughter Abigail, who are the reasons for all of my writing.

Foreword

Flannery O'Connor once wrote that an effective short story "successfully resists paraphrase." Likewise, the personal essay successfully resists classification. Despite the resurgence in popularity of the genre over the past twenty to thirty years, many readers still associate the word "essay" with the dry academic writing typically found in freshman composition texts. This is unfortunate, since there is a greater variety of voices in the genre than ever before. From the light, humorous writing of David Sedaris, to the thought-provoking essays of Sam Pickering, to the spiritually flavored writing of Anne Lamott, to the often indefinable work of Tom Wolfe, there is something for everyone in the personal essay. These and other writers have transformed the essay into a genre teeming with fresh ideas, intimate voices, and relevance to popular culture. Although they are still primarily published by university and regional presses, essays are also popular in publications ranging from *The New Yorker* to *Vanity Fair* and *The Atlantic Monthly* and every now and then, an essayist breaks through to the wider world and ends up on the best-seller list, much to the delight of those of us who love the form so much.

I've always been drawn to *reading* essays, but I often wondered what drew a person to want to *write* essays. I've come to the conclusion that an essay writer is someone who has reached a stage in life where he or she is ready to reflect—on hopes and dreams, both fulfilled and lost, on relationships, world views, the arts, politics–but now viewed through the lens of maturity, after significant life events have been distilled and are ready to be processed and bottled, and hopefully sold.

Perhaps we feel we have something to share that adheres to that golden rule of essay and memoir: it must be rooted in the personal, but also have a larger, universal theme or relevance. Perhaps we just want to record certain events, thoughts, and emotions before they are too far out of memory's grasp.

Or perhaps we just think we might be dead soon.

As a freelance writer, I have spent nearly thirty years writing articles on arts and entertainment for popular culture publications, and, while writing for those publications is a nice avocation, when I read the articles in *Script Magazine* or *American Profile* or *Bluegrass Unlimited,* I never feel the sense of delight that I get when I pick up a copy of *Ploughshares, Creative Nonfiction,* or *The Oxford American.*

I spent nearly two decades as a writing professor on the college level. During that time, I spent far too many hours reading dry-as-dust academic papers on the theory of teaching composition—ones rife with terms like "pedagogy" and "rubric" and "taxonomy," and loaded down with cumbersome statistics that often have little relevance to the real world of classroom teaching. With the academic essay, one must restrain from expressing too many opinions. With the personal essay, however, the gloves come off. As Joseph Epstein writes in his introduction to *The Norton Book of Personal Essays,* "all claims to objectivity are dropped at the outset, all masks removed, and the essayist proceeds with shameless subjectivity. . . Perhaps it is this intimacy that makes the personal essay an almost irresistible form."

In the essay, you can write about relatives, dead or living; you can admit to your prejudices, biases, personal struggles, and personal weaknesses. You can even curse if you want to.

When I was an undergraduate student in the early 1980s, it seemed the only essays that appeared in print were written by dead European white guys, the authors at the top of the literary sand pile, or the occasional celebrity. After all, who would want to read what a normal, everyday person would have to say about, well, anything? But then English teachers like Frank McCourt and Tobias Wolff, and Benedictine sisters like Kathleen Norris and journalists like Rick Bragg began turning out incredible memoirs, and the variety of voices continued to expand. Literary magazines began publishing personal essays more often, and the essay's "literary cousins"— reportage, memoir, and creative nonfiction—all seemed to enjoy a minor Renaissance of sorts also.

Robert Frost once said of poetry, "it begins in delight, and ends in wisdom," and I believe a well-written essay accomplishes the same. The personal essay, I have observed, often has a bittersweet or nostalgic tone. Maybe even one of regret. As the writer approaches the autumn of life, the reflections are often accompanied by a sense of loss: loss of youth, loss of simpler times, loss of friends, parents, or perhaps a loss of dreams. Take E.B. White's "Once More to the Lake," for instance. It is one of the most well crafted, but also one of the saddest, essays I've ever read.

Some of the greatest books of memoir in recent years concern the loss of a lover, loss of a parent or close friend, or the loss of memory (as with Floyd Skloot), or the loss of health, or loss of a way of life. I am approaching that period in my life when the inevitable progression begins: your friends' parents pass away, then your own parents pass away, then your friends start passing away, and eventually... well, it's your turn. As of this writing, I am still in my 50s, but I've lost nearly a dozen friends from high school over the past decade already, and nearly as many family members.

When I was a spry, young, 29-year old graduate student at Tennessee State University, I took a course in Shakespeare's Comedies taught by Dr. Wayne Billings, who related an event that occurred when he was about my age. After finishing his dissertation defense, Dr. Billings hopped on his bicycle for a spin around campus. The sun shone brightly and the world seemed to be his oyster ready for cracking as he looked forward to the start of his career, but for some odd reason, the specter of death hit him hard that day. Perhaps it was a Sylvia Plath-induced hangover or something similar. Dr. Billings shared with the class that for some odd reason that day, "death suddenly was no longer just a vague idea or abstract concept expressed by a bunch of poets, but suddenly something that might be within the realm of possibility for me as well!" We all got a chuckle from Dr. Billings' unique phrasing, and I forgot it for many years until recently, when out of the blue, death seemed within the realm of possibility for me as well. As a result, writing personal essays can serve as a form of therapy for this existential angst.

So it is with these feelings that I complete my first collection of personal essays: on the one hand, I am thrilled that a portion of my life has been captured and recorded in written form, but on the other, I feel a bereavement at the loss of so many people and places dear to me. When I began the essay "Clay," my father was still alive. I have written at least a dozen more drafts since his passing in 2009, born partly out of respect for the dead, as well as from a renewed perspective of his life, seeing it as a whole rather than just focusing on the unfortunate mid-life crisis that he seemed to experience in his 50s and 60s. Several other essays in the collection, after sitting for a few years, seemed to have "distilled" to the point where they are ready to be corked and shipped.

Another endearing aspect of the personal essay is its ability to provide us an opportunity to sneak a peek into the lives of others, and to allow them a chance to peer into ours. Thank you for being willing to take a peek at a little corner of my world, through the essays in *Disposable Thoughts*. I am honored that you took the time to do so.

Table of Contents

A QUIET, WELL-LIGHTED PLACE

It is a crisp, clear October morning, and I am sitting on the deck of a condominium far above the town of Blowing Rock in the highlands of western North Carolina. The condo is perched on the side of a mountain at roughly 3,000 feet elevation. From where I sit, I can see the rippling ridges of the glorious Cherokee National Forrest, Grandfather Mountain, the nearby town of Boone, and several peaks in the distance. The cars making their descent down Route 105 into Boone look like little Hot Wheels cars.

Here, at the higher elevations, the edges of the leaves on the maples, oaks, and poplars that envelope this leg of the Appalachian range are already morphing into the brilliant gold, magenta and orange hues that will remain for the next two to three weeks, before they begin their autumn ballet that will guide them to the forest floor below. The only sound I can hear at this height is the periodic hum of a distant leaf blower from somewhere down the mountain, and the intermittent whisper of the wind through the pines.

The Plexiglas banister of the balcony where I now sit affords me a panoramic view of the surrounding mountains.

To my left, on a peak perhaps ten miles away and over 6000 feet in elevation, there is a collection of dark gray cumulous clouds obscuring the summit, possibly sprinkling the top of the mountain with an early dusting of snow, but the rest of the sky around me is blue and clear. According to the thermometer on the deck, it is 60 degrees.

Scents of caramel flavor from my steaming cup of coffee and a freshly baked apple cinnamon muffin waft past my nose as a large hawk, not 50 feet away from me, hangs in the updraft literally suspended in mid-air like Michael Jordan over the free throw lane. He watches me write for several seconds before he banks to his right and begins his slow descent down the mountain.

When I finally run out of steam tonight, I plan to take myself out for a steak dinner and a glass of Merlot at a restaurant in Blowing Rock. After that, a pint of Ben and Jerry's Peach Cobbler, a DVD of *Ocean's 11*, and a long soak in the hot tub await me upon my return; afterwards I will sleep deeply, rise in the morning, and start writing again.

So perched on the side of the mountain that weekend, with nothing but my laptop and my coffee—no papers to grade, no students knocking on my door, no cable, no texts, no telephones—I am finally able to focus like Einstein and complete a number of well-written pages, if I have to say so myself.

But what happens when I have to go back to the real world below? What then? As the years go by, it is becoming increasingly more challenging to find a quiet place to write in a noisy world. Real authors, the ones who crank out one or more books a year for decades sometimes tell me I will never get anything written if I need a place like the one in Boone to get my work done. The late E.B. White was one such scribe. "A writer who waits for ideal conditions under which to work," he wrote, "will die without putting a word on paper."

Although my output of writing may pale in comparison to many professional writers, over the past twenty-five years, I have completed two masters' theses, and perhaps 400 academic and popular culture articles and essays. I've written who knows how many papers for graduate classes. I've edited two music anthologies, written and produced an hour-long PBS documentary, written one full-length memoir, two unpublished fiction novels (both of which were lost in a house fire ten years ago), lyrics to perhaps a hundred songs, dozens of television scripts, three screenplays, and one essay collection. To do this, I've always needed a quiet, well-lighted place where I can focus in order to be productive, and the barriers to my finding one border on the conspiratorial. And the digital age is making it more and more challenging. A few miles from my home just east of Nashville, on a road with sparse traffic, there is a Shell gas station. I have noticed while using the lavatory there how perfectly quiet and well lit it is, and I am seriously considering calling the corporate office to see if I may lease the space.

William Zinsser, author of the memoir, *Writing Places*, mixes advice on the craft of writing while describing the various environments, from noisy newsrooms, to his office in a flat in Manhattan, to his college offices and other locales where he wrote over a span of nearly seventy years.

After working for magazines and newspapers for many years, Zinsser wrote about the daunting experience of going out on his own for the first time. Zinsser had a wife and a family and was then living on East 86th Street on the Upper East Side of Manhattan. "So began 11 years of sitting alone in a small room, the only sound the clatter of my typewriter," Zinsser wrote. "I thought back to my *Herald Tribune* days when we all made regular trips to the water cooler—far more than our kidneys required; it was our own little village green. Now all that was gone. What had I done?" Zinsser added, "I'm a social person, dependent on people and on talk, however small. Now overnight, I had no place to go. Nobody to exchange ideas with, no paycheck or pension or support system. I would have to be my own support system, skating out on the thin ice of self-employment."

Zinsser of course, became quite prolific, authoring 19 books and perhaps thousands of articles and essays, and even found time to teach at Yale for several years before his passing in 2015. But I wonder if even Zinsser would have been as productive had the Internet and social media been around when he began his career. The first decade of the new millennium ushered in a whole new era of distraction with the advent of social media. I recently heard the term "digital dementia" to describe a very real malady that causes us to lose our ability to focus for extended periods of time, which some ascribe to texting and social media. This distraction not only affects critical thinking, but also creative thinking. The social media pundits tell us that in order to be effective marketers, business people, professors, or authors, we must constantly be engaged with our "tribe," whether that be students, readers, or our professional colleagues. We are basically never permitted to shut down, or log off or we risk being branded as unprofessional or novices.

Jesus warned us against this obsession with busy-ness over 2000 years ago, in the New Testament story of Martha and Mary. Martha was very busy doing things for Jesus, while Mary just wanted to sit at his feet and listen. When Martha chastised Mary, Jesus said Mary had chosen the better thing.

On a recent trip to California, someone offered me a free book on Kabala. In the book, one of the chapters discusses what it terms "the adversary." Some people interpret this to be Satan, but the book seems to suggest that it can also be anything—people, things, or circumstances—that keeps us from staying focused on our higher purpose. Clearly, I have had more than my share of "adversaries" sent into my life to disrupt me from my calling. One of them was named Wilma. In fact, I have had a number of "Wilmas" in my life.

The first Wilma was an elderly, widowed secretary at a community college where I taught English for many years. Because the school was so quiet on the weekends, I often went to my office to work on my freelance writing and book projects. As an instructor of writing, I typically had a course load of three sections of basic composition (with 20 to 25 students in each) and two survey literature courses (also with about 20-25 students). The requisite grading, class preparation, and reading required to teach these courses was at least a 40-hour a week job, not including the time it took to do advising, attend faculty committee work, answer emails, attend conferences and the never-ending array of meetings on everything from the Visiting Writers Series to department budgets to calendar committees. While there, I began to feel more like Mr. Holland in *Mr. Holland's Opus*: that the myriad tasks required of professors would prohibit me from ever being able to write anything.

The first couple of weekends were sheer bliss. But I became distraught when I discovered that Wilma, the secretary whose desk was in an open-air suite right next to my office, would also often come in on weekends. Although she only came in for a couple of hours, she had an uncanny ability to get there at the precise time that I would arrive. If I came in from 8 a.m. to noon, Wilma would come in at the same time. If I waited until noon and worked until 4, she would do the same. If I got in without her spotting me, I'd shut my door and try to hide out so she would not engage me in the constant chit-chat and office gossip she was prone to spout, but inevitably nature would call, or I would scrape a chair or pull a book from a shelf and I would hear Wilma barking, "Who's in there?" Sometimes I tried to play deaf, but she would come banging on my door and I knew she had found me out.

One of the other "Wilmas" turned out to be my own daughter. When I finally broke to writing full-time myself, I set up a home office. I had received a modest book advance, and had another part-time salary as an adjunct professor at a small Catholic college. My wife was working part-time, and I was receiving a steady flow of freelance work as well. We did the math and, since we live modestly, figured we could survive on these sources of income, which would leave at least 25 hours a week to work on some book and documentary projects I had in the hopper.

So at last, there I was. A home office with very little overhead, a nest egg in the bank, and several major projects to work on, with enough monthly income to cover the basics, and a quiet place where I could focus. A dream for every writer, right?

At least, when Abigail was not around.

At the time, she was about 7, and cute as a kitten. She has always had an easy-going temperament and a sweet spirit, and there were many mornings when I would be on a roll, and hear a light tapping on my door. She would open it softly, and ask me quietly if I could come have a snack with her or play a game with her. Her name means "father's joy" and she always has been. She is our only child, and I tried to give her plenty of quality time in the evenings, but I also hated to stop writing when I was on a roll. Still, who could resist a sweet offer like this? The days when children are that cute are so fleeting, so I seldom resisted her offers, even though I would become frustrated at myself later for breaking my flow.

I later discovered an unoccupied corner office in a nearby insurance building that was for rent. It was cheap, and didn't require any long-term contracts, so I moved my office desk and chair, a lamp stand, a couple of bookcases, and an old couch from my bonus room, and set up shop there. Again, I was in writing nirvana.

There, the next "Wilma" entered my life.

Initially, the office suite next to me was vacant, until a rental management company moved in. One of the employees, whose name I can't recall, was a large, older woman who was in charge of collecting the rents each month. Every morning, I heard a voice bellowing through the thin walls between the suites, "No, it's due by the tenth. No, the *tenth*! It's always been the tenth. No, it can't be mailed. It has to be in the office!" The majority of their renters must have been hard of hearing.

Two years after that, I went to work as a writer/producer for a network television show with a magazine format, and I was given a nice quiet office on the second floor of a production studio that once housed a Sam's Club. Each morning, I would drop my daughter at school about 7:00 a.m. on my way to work, and would arrive at the office shortly after, a full hour and a half before most of the staff would arrive. For several weeks, I used this time to work on some of my book and screenplay projects, but it wasn't long before the next "Wilma" came into my life.

The production manager was the only other employee in the office who arrived early, and I spent several months hiding away from him in my office until one day when he discovered that I got there most mornings about the same time. While I typed away on screenplays and essays, he would often find reasons to interrupt me with his phone calls, emails, and an occasional knock on the door to give me updates on my segments, my expense reports, office gossip, and any other matter that would take me out of the flow.

No matter where I tried to hide and write, there was always a "Wilma" there to distract me. Was this simply one of the crosses I was to bear in this life?

William Powers wrote of our pervasive cultural distraction in his book, *Hamlet's Blackberry* (written before I-Phones and I-Pads ousted the Blackberry as the preferred choice of mobile device). According to Powers, "By some estimates, recovering focus can take ten to twenty times the length of the interruption. So a one-minute interruption could require fifteen minutes of recovery time."

These days, it seems that friends or colleagues interpret turning off your phone or logging off as a personal affront. If we don't return a text within a few seconds or minutes, let alone a few hours, the likelihood of offending the sender is quite high. At one time, we could claim we were in dead spots, but through the efforts of the cellular carriers, there are few places left on the planet, save for maybe some in the Congo or in the rain forest or the Sahara, that are out of range, so that excuse is no longer valid. I've already pulled the "I was on a missions trip to Africa" card several times this year, but nobody is buying it anymore.

Should it really be this hard?

I wish I could be like J.K. Rowling, who I hear wrote the bulk of her first *Harry Potter* book on a commuter train while working as a single mother.

I attended the Southern Festival of Books in Nashville recently to listen to a panel, which included Rick Bragg, a Pulitzer-prize winning author. The members were discussing their writing habits. During the discussion, Bragg scoffed at the notion that writers need certain places or circumstances to focus on their writing. "I've written on tops of barrels out in the oil fields, and in the Middle East with soldiers around and bullets whizzing past me," Bragg said. "I can't afford to wait for the muse to land on me. No real writer can."

Bragg spoke of conducting writing workshops where he would hear "sweet little ladies" talking to each other about how the muse failed to land on them and they couldn't get any writing done. Bragg said we have to tell the muse what to do, not vice versa. Given his track record, it's hard to argue. Perhaps I just need to admit I will never be a real writer on the level of a Rick Bragg, and pursue a career in real estate, even if it means spending all of my mornings shouting to a hearing impaired person, "No, it's due by the *tenth*!"

While there have been times when I have knocked out a few good pages at my favorite Panera Bread Company, with the whir of blenders and babies crying surrounding me, those moments are few and far between. Most of the time in these circumstances, I spend much of my time just staring out the window.

This culture of distraction has even invaded academia, where deep thinking is supposed to be valued, but still is often viewed with suspicion, Between advising students, filling out attendance sheets withdrawal forms, financial aid forms, disability disclosures, outcomes and objectives, creating syllabi, updating course websites or "shells," texting and tweeting, I always had trouble finding focus time for writing and thinking, once primary activities for academicians.

Reading can even be suspect in an academic environment. Once while sitting in my office at a community college where I was teaching, I heard one student in the hallway remark to another who was on his way in to see me, "Go on in. He ain't doing nuttin' but readin'."

Reading, thinking, cogitating, even staring can be great warm-up activities for writing. Joyce Carol Oates once wrote, "I have always spent most of my time staring out the window, noting what is there, daydreaming, or brooding."

A fellow Nashvillian, author Ann Patchett, also thinks highly of staring. In her published speech to the 2008 graduating class at her alma mater, Sarah Lawrence College entitled, *What Now?* Patchett cautions potential writers who may think of the writing life as filled with glamour and celebrity. "I would say that my yearly intake of glamour averages out to be about one hour a month, and that includes giving speeches," Ann writes. "As far as the rest of my time, the activity that I am most likely to be engaged in is staring. If staring ever becomes an Olympic event, I'll be bringing home the gold. While other people go to work. I stare out the window. I stare at my dog. I stare at little pieces of paper and paragraphs and single sentences and a buzzing computer screen." And who am I to argue with the woman who wrote *Bel Canto*? If she says I need to stare, I'm going to stare!

Franz Kafka said of solitude, "You do not need to leave your room. Remain sitting at your table and listen. Do not even listen. Simply wait, be quiet, still and solitary. The world will freely offer itself to you to be unmasked. It has no choice; it will roll in ecstasy at your feet." And Blaise Pascal wrote, "All men's miseries derive from not being able to sit in a quiet room alone."

Reading, thinking, journaling, staring—all can be great warm-up exercises prior to writing. I like to use the analogy of a marathon runner to illustrate how challenging it can be when one desires long periods of uninterrupted silence to write, but gets interrupted frequently. To prepare for a race, the runner stocks up on carbs the night before, then spends half an hour or so in the morning stretching, then jogging a mile or two to warm up before the race even begins. Even then, it's not until the fifth or sixth mile, according to the marathon runners I've known, that the runner really hits his stride. But imagine a runner being stopped every two to three miles in the middle of a marathon, just to chat. How distracting would that be? That's the way it feels for writers when taken out of the "flow." And it happens a lot.

Perhaps the experience I had on the mountaintop in Carolina is just a false nirvana that does not really exist in the everyday world, so I should just stop looking for it. Then again, there is always the Harper Lee or J.D. Salinger approach: write one great book and retire. It doesn't even have to be great literature; just one good commercially successful book. I'll settle for a *Life's Little Instruction Book* if it sells five million copies!

In the future, when I have trouble focusing or being productive, maybe I'll just tell myself that I am ruminating over the next *To Kill a Mockingbird* or *Catcher in the Rye*. And for the times when I am feeling inspired and productive, well, the restroom at the Shell station is looking better and better all the time.

CUTTING THE CORD

I've never asked a doctor to substitute teach for me, so imagine my surprise when I was asked to perform the first surgery on my daughter. Oh sure, I loved the board game Operation as a kid. Didn't we all? But the only recompense for screwing up with the game was a loud buzzer and the humiliation of knowing my big brother had won. I sensed the stakes might be a little higher with actual surgery.

The morning of March 29, 2001, at Vanderbilt University Medical Center in Nashville, after 14 hours in the delivery room awaiting the arrival of Abigail Jane Rudder, my wife and I were both exhausted.

Her contractions had slowed around 6:00 a.m. and then nearly halted. Our daughter's stubbornness was already beginning to manifest, and she hadn't even been born yet. It was as if she were telling us, *"It's nice and warm in here. If you want me, you're going to have to come in and get me."*

We had been warned of all the dangers of caesarian sections in our Bradley Method birthing class, which we had attended together during the previous three months. As a result, my wife was dead set against it unless, quite literally, her life depended on it. She toughed it out until the last few hours but began to grow weak and had little energy left to push.

Thinking the worst was over, I stepped out into the parking garage to have a celebratory cigar, as every new father is supposed to do. (Nothing like the smell of cigar smoke mixed with exhaust fumes at 7:00 a.m. to get the blood flowing.) I was under the impression that, by the time I extinguished my $10 stogie, all of the yelling, the blood, the gore and the assorted other unpleasantries of the birthing room would have ceased and I could arrive just in time to hold my freshly scrubbed, little baby burrito in my arms. Moments later, I was summoned back to the birthing room. To my surprise I discovered that we were now no closer than when I had left.

"What do we do, now?" I asked Lori, our midwife, a pleasant, young, blond woman in her mid-thirties with boundless energy, who had been with us nearly the entire time.

"Well, you have two choices. We can let your wife get some rest. Then we can give her just a little Pitocin to see if that can move things alone a little."

"Kind of like a birth laxative, huh?" I interjected.

"I guess," she replied hesitantly. "But if that doesn't happen and Clare is too tired to push anymore, we may have to start thinking about the C-section." The very word took me back to the memories of our birthing class.

The woman who led our Bradley class was a woman I called The Birth Nazi. She was probably in her early 50s, with slightly graying hair that was often pulled up in a bun reminiscent of a Mennonite. She was a big-boned woman, over six feet tall, and wore the kind of 1950s-style glasses that my second grade teacher, Mrs. DuMolin, used to wear. She seldom wore makeup and would not tolerate tardiness, absenteeism, talking during the videos, or gum chewing.

During the three months of classes, held once a week, the Birth Nazi must have shown the video of a live birth at least eight times. I failed to see the usefulness of viewing this spectacle more than once and often found myself sneaking off to the bathroom once the crowning began. If I were caught looking at anything remotely similar to this on the Internet, my wife would have hit me in the head with a frying pan, but for some reason, my staring at a strange, naked woman spread-eagled on a hospital bed for an hour every Tuesday night was supposed to do wonderful things for our marriage.

I always tried to get a seat as close to the restroom as I could. I think the Birth Nazi caught on to the fact that my bladder would call at the exact same time every week, so she began guarding the door. In the dark of her living room with the video images flickering on the television set and the other six couples sitting with us on the floor, I would start fidgeting, then inch my way toward the door, and finally make my escape. One night as I went through my ritual and the others were still mesmerized by the television, I snuck out.

She was right there waiting. "Get back in there," she said.

"Come on, it's the same thing we saw last week," I whined. "I know how it ends."

She unfolded her arms and pointed toward the living room.

"OK," I said meekly like a schoolboy who was just caught taking an extra chocolate milk for lunch.

"I'm just not used to seeing that much blood," I ushered one last protest as I went back in the living room, "especially right after dinner."

Over the next ten weeks, we were treated to all sorts of helpful information about the "intervention spiral"—the series of unfortunate occurrences that might take place should we try to circumvent nature and attempt to speed up the process with modern medical technology. I can't remember all of the possible consequences that we were warned of, but it seems that the potential side effects included everything from a lopsided baby head (due to the pressure of the forceps) to abdominal distension, halitosis and nail fungus.

The couples in our class came from quite a variety of backgrounds. One young lady had been raised on The Farm, a famous hippie commune in Summertown, Tennessee, about an hour south of Nashville. The Farm was settled in 1973 by 300 San Francisco hippies who began raising organic crops, built a school, and started a book publishing company there. The Farm was also famous for its tradition of midwifery and natural childbirth for all the hippie kids. Like many children of The Farm, however, this young lady had rejected the rustic, cloistered farm life of her parents in exchange for a modern, relatively comfortable, conservative life in the suburbs, but held on to some of the ideals of that generation nevertheless.

Others in the class included chiropractors, music business executives, salespeople, and teachers. Many of the women in our class were planning on home births, but we weren't quite ready to go that far.

The first thing they tell you in a Lamaze or Bradley birthing class is that there is a high probability that, when the actual contractions begin, you will probably freak out and forget everything you've learned—especially the man.

I am proud to say I was able to confirm that.

We learned that we should start thinking about calling the hospital when the contractions were about five to ten minutes apart. I thought an hour apart sounded like a safer window, though. I had heard tales of couples waiting a little too long and then having to deliver their children in the back seat of a car along the Interstate, and that prospect did not bode well. After all, how can you boil water with a cigarette lighter adapter?

Against Clare's protestations, I rushed her to the labor and delivery suite at Vanderbilt, where they sent us home after about ten minutes. "But don't you want to keep her here for a while just to make sure?" I begged. "They might start speeding up any minute."

"Mr. Rudder, those are Braxton-Hicks contractions. It's false labor," the attending nurse said. "Your baby is not due for three or four more days."

Sensing that I was fighting a losing battle, we packed up our stuff and left.

At home, I was a basket case. In bed, my wife's body would shudder every hour on the hour. The little mini-convulsions were fascinating, and so regular I began setting the clocks in the house to them. I watched her as she slept (or rather, tried sleep). It was mesmerizing to watch—almost like a dance move. It started out around her knees, kind of slow, then quickly worked its way up her legs and then into her back, as she shimmied faster. It was almost as if someone had just poured ice down her back.

"Are *those* contractions? I poked her gently.

"No, sweetie. That's the false labor she was referring to."

"If you're nine months pregnant, how do you know the difference between the real ones and the fake ones?"

"The real ones are more intense and they come more regularly," she yawned. "Now I need some rest."

She was taking this way too calmly.

This went on for three more days. In the meantime, I took a sleeping bag to work and caught catnaps between classes since I wasn't sleeping much at night. Clare didn't seem to mind the waiting.

Finally, she told me she thought the real contractions had begun, so we packed up and headed to the hospital again. It was on a Sunday afternoon, as I recall. This time it *was* for real, and they checked us into the hospital. Early in the morning, Clare began to get really fatigued. That's when our midwife started using the "C" word again, but we kept believing things would start moving soon.

For some reason, there were a lot of people in our birthing when the actual delivery started, but that didn't seem to bother my wife. There was a midwife, an OBGY doctor, two nurses, three medical students, and I think a reporter from the *Tennessean* newspaper or something. Not sure what he was doing there.

When she finally began pushing hard, I was standing behind my wife's head—there was too big of a crowd at her feet—and I saw all the bright blood and space alien-like matter that I had seen in the videos in the birthing class all over again. I knew there also had to be a baby somewhere in that mix. All the while, Clare continued to push. Finally, a little after 8:00 a.m., Abigail stuck out the white flag and surrendered. We were parents. That's when the midwife handed me the knife and said, "So, do you want to cut the umbilical cord?"

I was speechless. Everyone in the room went silent and they all stared at me. "Is that really, um, the protocol?" I wondered if they were going to ask me if I wanted to eat the afterbirth, like Tom Cruise claimed he did.

She told me lots of men did it. "Well, OK," I said as I reached out to take the knife.

There are certain times in a man's life when he has to simply face his fears and prove that he can overcome them, when he can take up his manhood, summon his courage, face the mythical dragon in the archetypal hero's journey, and slay it once and for all.

This was not one of those times.

"I don't know. I'm a little shaky from being up most of the night," I said, handing her back the knife. "How about if you do it and I'll watch? Then, when our next baby is born, I'll be all set."

I watched as she took the knife back and began to cut the cord that had been the lifeline from my daughter to my wife's body for the past nine months. This crimson-covered tube of flesh had been the provider of all the nourishment my daughter needed for the previous nine months. It had provided oxygen, water, and nutrients. It had served as the emotional and psychological bond between the two. And now it was going to be severed.

After Abigail took her first scream, they cleaned her up and handed her to me. All of our well-meaning friends had told me if I got the chance to cut the cord and did not take advantage, I would regret it. I recall having no such feeling, then or now. I simply looked at the beautiful, wrinkly, little ball of flesh they handed me with a sense of wonder and awe, and tried to think of something profound to say. But all that came to mind was, "Welcome to the world, A.J. But I gotta tell you, though—it's all uphill from here, kiddo."

DISPOSABLE THOUGHTS

"What've you got to show for it,
Willie? Put your hands on it."

FROM DEATH OF A SALESMAN

"We're in the air business," Tom Wolfe once said of the writing profession. This was, of course, long before the Internet and Kindles and Nooks, but today his words seem more relevant than ever.

Even before the digital age, writers had to live with the fact that only a small portion of their writings would ever make their way through the labyrinthine publishing world to see the light of a bookstore or magazine stand. And even from there, many are sent back to the publisher as returns. It's easy to understand Andy Warhol's line about everybody being famous for fifteen minutes, because that is about the average shelf life of a book in a bookstore before it is whisked back to the publisher for a credit. And, according to one study I read recently, only about a third of the books that are purchased and taken home are read all the way through.

And now, to deal us the final blow of impermanence, along comes the digital age, making our work even more transient. Many are predicting that within the next decade, we will be a paperless society. It has not come to pass, although we are getting closer. Marketing guru Seth Godin recently published an article entitled, "The End of Paper," which only confirms my fears. And the nebulous area of electronic storage where many of our files are kept is even referred to as "the cloud."

My wife and I both have a "green" side: we recycle, drive fuel-efficient cars, and try to leave a small carbon footprint. I realize that purchasing more e-books would be better for the environment, but doggone it—I still like my paper books. I like touching the cover, and I like ruffling through the pages, and going to book signings where the author actually picks up a pen and writes something to me inside the cover.

Reading will always be a physical, tactile experience, and paper books will be my primary medium for the foreseeable future. Furthermore, like Mark Twain's death. I believe the rumors of the demise of physical books have been greatly exaggerated. A recent statistic indicated that of the tens of millions of Kindles and Nooks purchased in recent years, a full 60% of owners had yet to download a book, instead using the device to simply play games or surf the Net.

Consider the modern bookstore. It is meant to be a multi-sensory experience: from the colorful posters advertising recent bestsellers, to the colorful graphics on the book covers, the soft jazz playing on the intercom, the wafting scents of freshly brewed coffee wafting through the stores. True readers don't just want more information; they want their senses stimulated. They want to touch, feel, taste, and smell the bookstore, not just to visit it. Maybe they even want to interact with other human beings after staring at a computer all day.

When I saw my first e-Book reader, perhaps sometime around 2005 or '06, I reacted much the way a songwriter may have reacted the first time he heard about Napster. *Are they serious?* I thought. *This thing is going to replace my bookshelf?* The thought of taking it to a beach on a sunny day, worrying about the sand getting into the circuit board, as well the difficulty viewing the screen, did not comfort me. Imagine trying to read the *Brothers Karamazov* on this, I thought. Of course, like most Americans my age, I have since succumbed to the readers. After many months of walking past them at Office Depot and Best Buy, glancing at them as they stared back, wet-lipped, enticing me, I finally fell into sin and now I own a Kindle Fire, too. But no matter the power and thrill of their allure, I'll always leave this temporary mistress and go back to the humble and true affections of my first love— my paperbound books—to which I have pledged my eternal commitment.

In my mind, books were meant to be held, to be dog-eared and pulled off a shelf at leisure—not turned on or booted up. Being forced to choose between the two formats reminds me of being in a public restroom where you have the option of drying your hands with the electronic blower that sounds like a 747 landing or grabbing a paper towel. Screw the landfills. I still want a paper towel.

It probably seems anathema to the millennials who were raised in an almost totally digital world that even today, someone wakes up across town in Nashville about 3:00 a.m., travels miles to a printing press on the north side of town, fills up his car with copies of the Nashville *Tennessean* newspaper or the *New York Times,* as newspapers carriers everywhere have done for hundreds of years, wraps them in plastic, and drops them in my and my neighbors' driveways, where we retrieve them to be consumed with a cup of French roast each Sunday morning.

And the crazy thing is, I look forward to it, and often read them cover-to-cover! How many articles from the *Tennessean* have I read online over the past several years? A dozen at most.

When I travel for work, one of the most pleasant experiences of hotel life is being able to open my hotel door each morning to find a hard copy of *USA Today* waiting for me and I read that too, sometimes, cover to cover. How many online articles have I read on the *USA Today* website? I can't think of one. Yes, even today, 600 years after Gutenberg invented the offset printing press, people still print and distribute hard copies of newspapers.

And I, for one, still like it.

As a child growing up in the tiny river town of Wellsville, Ohio, one of my favorite memories of Garfield Elementary School, was the day the *Weekly Reader* paperbacks arrived.

I can still see Mrs. DuMolin, my third grade teacher, passing around a catalogue and order forms to her students. A few weeks later, the books would mysteriously appear at our door. This whole world of book publishing, printing, and distribution mystified me. (Four decades later, it *still* mystifies me.)

When I was a small boy, my mother worked as a waitress. My father quit school in the ninth grade and worked most of his life mining clay, but they were both readers, and they valued education. I'm sure it was hard on them, but they somehow came up with an extra fifty cents or a dollar so we could buy a couple of paperbacks from the *Weekly Reader* book club. Unlike the loaner books we got from the city's public school system, these books were *ours*. We could take them home and read them any time we wanted—even during the summer.

When they came—usually on a Friday, if my memory serves—Mrs. DuMolin would open the large UPS carton and pass out the books, still wrapped in cellophane, along with our paid receipts and original order forms. They felt so pristine after we moved the wrappers. The brightly colored covers had photos of exotic people and places. I ran my fingers across them, feeling the glossy exteriors and smelling the fresh ink before tucking them in my Batman lunch box and taking them home for the weekend. Although I was physically active as a child, I often would look forward to a rainy weekend, so I could lie in bed and read. Lying there in that little three-bedroom house on Chester Avenue, I was instantly transported to other worlds.

When I read about Frederick Douglas and the Underground Railroad, I thought of the huge Victorian homes on Riverside Avenue in Wellsville that, according to local folklore, had once been part of the Railroad. When I read about Anne Frank hiding out in a closet in Amsterdam, I would have trouble sleeping, or would have dreams that the Nazis were after me. One book, a sports anthology, was a collection of strange but true stories from the sports world, including the story of "Wrong Way" Riegels, the University of California player who, in the 1929 Rose Bowl, scooped up a fumble and returned it 65 yards to the wrong end zone. Another story told of the annihilation of Cumberland College in Lebanon, Tennessee—just a few miles from where I now sit writing this essay—at the hands of Georgia Tech in 1915 in the most lopsided victory in sports history, a 222-0 drubbing in which Tech scored on every possession.

That was one of my favorites, but my all-time favorite book was the one about a small boy and a runaway slave and their adventures rafting down a river, not unlike the one that flowed just a few blocks from my home. When I read the opening lines, I knew this was a character I could relate to: "You don't about me, without you have read a book by the name of *The Adventures of Tom Sawyer*, but that ain't no matter. That book was made by a Mister Mark Twain, and he told the truth mainly . . . with some stretchers."

I've been in love with words ever since.

I have noticed over the years that the concept of putting our thoughts on paper or a computer screen as a means of vocation, or even an avocation, seems to strike people of other professions as an odd thing for some reason. While re-financing our mortgage recently, I was reminded of how curious a profession writing it is to many people. One of the things the new mortgage guidelines require is an intense scrutiny of any extra income going into or out of one's bank accounts. Our mortgage broker, upon perusing our recent checking statements, began inquiring as to the source of all of these two, three, and five-hundred-dollar deposits into our account. When he interrogated me further, perhaps thinking that I was laundering money for Al Qaeda or the mob, the conversation went something like this:

"So what are these extra deposits?"

"They're from different publications. I'm a copywriter."

"Oh, so you write the ads?"

"No, not the ads. I provide content. You know the little squiggly black marks in between all the pretty pictures."

"Oh, funny," he said, but was clearly not amused. "So are you a sports writer or something?"

"Not sports. Sometimes I cover arts and entertainment, but I also write opinion pieces and essays."

"Essays?" he asked. Now that really threw him. "Like in a college textbook?

"Kind of."

"They pay people for that?" he chuckled.

"Some do. For others, it's just to build up your clips and get a byline."

"Clips?" he queried.

"Yeah, well …never mind …" For the life of me, I could not understand why this was so hard to grasp.

"So are you a part-time employee or something? Do you get a regular paycheck? Are you on a salary?" he asked.

"No. There are good months and there are slow months. Just whenever I can sell an editor on an idea."

"I see. So do you have a P & L statement?"

"A what?"

"A profit and loss statement? You know, a spread sheet?"

"Well, there isn't much overhead once you buy a laptop. When I get paid, I just throw the check stub into a shoe box and add it all up at the end of the year."

"I see," he said. "What about assets and liabilities?"

"No."

"A monthly cash flow chart?"

"No."

He sighed. I was beginning to think he worked for the IRS.

"Quarterly or yearly income projections?"

"No. But I do sit down on New Year's Eve and jot down some goals for the year."

"Sounds like a helluva way to run a business," he said.

"It's not like any other business. You don't have employees, or office space, or equipment or those kinds of things. You just kind of sit down and bang out your ideas and try to sell them. I get paid, you know . . . for my … words, ideas, for my thoughts," I finally said, feeling the need to reduce the concept to its simplest form. "I write the words down and send it to them, and they send me a check."

"Ideas?" he said. "You get paid for ideas? Thoughts? And opinions? Boy that must be nice," he chortled. "If my wife could get paid for that, we'd both be rich! So do you have any samples of your work?"

"I have some. But others, well, a lot of the websites I have written for are actually..." I trailed off.

"Are what?"

"A lot are offline now, so the links might not be live. They have probably been...uh...deleted."

I felt as though I were being cross-examined in a murder trial. And I wasn't making a good case for myself.

"Well," he said, closing the folder, "I'll see if we can get you qualified without it, but the underwriter might need to see some more evidence," he said.

That's when it hit me. *Tom Wolfe was right. I really am in the air business*! The construction worker can stand back and proudly view his edifice. The painter can see his vision manifested in vibrant colors and hues on the canvas. Even the autoworker can watch the work of his hands drive off the assembly line. But what have we got? At least before the digital age, we could hold up a book, something tangible, with the hope that some of our writings, our thoughts, might actually outlast us. A little piece of immortality, if you will. But no longer.

And if we go to a totally paperless society, what will we have then? As Willie Loman's brother Ben asked him, "What have you got, Willie? Put your hands on it."

Can we put our hands on it? An electronic file? A thumb drive? All of our life's work reduced to an electronic sequence of 0's and 1's that can be deleted with the stroke of a key, or dragged to the trash bin with a mouse on a Mac. Our daily outpouring of heart and soul now, with apologies to Kansas, will be so much dust in the binary wind.

Perhaps there is something vaguely Freudian about it, but I resent the idea of holding up a two-inch thumb drive as the only physical representation of my years of hard work. No, I fear that we are going the way of disposable razors and cigarette lighters. Our ideas, our words, our inspirations, our thoughts—will be read and then disposed of with a click of a mouse or the stroke of a key on a keypad, and my nightmare will have come to pass.

Borders Books is now but a quaint memory, and chains like Barnes and Noble and Lifeway are hanging on by a thread, surviving on the income from the greeting cards and toys, no doubt. Still, I have to believe this brave new digital world will have a place for paper, for libraries and for bookstores, where I can still browse the isles, feel the books, smell the coffee and pastries.

In *Hamlet*, Prince Hamlet observes sarcastically that his mother seems to be over her husband's passing within "these two hours."

"Nay, 'tis twice two months, my lord," Ophelia replies. To which young Hamlet retorts, "So long? Well, then there's hope that a great man's memory may outlive his life half a year!"

Although I don't view myself as a "great man," I would like to think that my memory night outlast my life at least half a year. The chances of that happening will be vastly increased if there are still physical books and libraries and bookstores.

At least, it would be some tangible evidence of my time spent here—a literary tombstone if you will—and a small legacy that, unlike this frail and mortal frame, might not be so disposable.

FALLUJAH

(Originally published in *The Pinch*, University of Memphis)

A gentle rain began to fall on Nashville, Tennessee the day the insurgents first stepped up their attacks in Fallujah.

That morning, the *New York Times* ran a front page story with a photo of the bodies of four innocent U.S. civilians—contractors—their charred torsos hanging from a bridge like smoked hams. Even more disturbing than the images of the mangled corpses were photos of Iraqi children and ebullient young men as they stood around the bodies, whacking the corpses with sticks, grabbing shoes and belts for souvenirs.

According to the *Times* story, someone had spread a rumor that the four were clandestine CIA agents. After the car the contractors were driving was hit with an RPG and exploded, the men inside who were still alive tried to flee the flaming vehicle, but were set upon like wounded antelopes on the Serengeti and ripped to pieces before becoming bridge adornments high above the Euphrates.

The photos were such a stark contrast to the ones that beamed across the globe just months before, the Iraqis dancing in the streets, liberated from their oppressor like the flying monkeys in the *Wizard of Oz* freed from the Wicked Witch of the West. How could these have been the same Iraqis that had just cheered U.S. troops entering Baghdad and, assisted by marines, toppled the statues of Hussein in the center of the city? Did this new turn of events truly reflect the prevailing sentiment of the entire country, or only that of a small group of former Baathists or Al Qaeda members trying to prevent the new government from taking power? For many in the U.S., it was the first sign of many to come that this may have been a mistake.

After I finish the *Times* story, I wander into the backyard of my home, located in a quiet suburb east of Nashville. I am deep in thought as my three-year-old daughter Abigail follows me. As the rain sputters off and on, Abigail tells me she wants to race me to the hollow log in the backyard, so off we go. After three sprints to the tree, she is winded and falls down, laughing the infectious laughter only a three-year-old is capable of. The kind of laughter that knows nothing of Fallujah or Basra, or Afghanistan, or the Sudan, or North Korea—or even North Nashville, for that matter. Her world is the freshly cut grass on the backyard lawn, and animal crackers at Sunday school, Big Bird and Elmo, and mama's warm hugs in the night when her tummy hurts.

Right now, I want to enter that world, if just for a moment. I like it better than mine.

We walk along the drainage ditch to the neighbor who has a goldfish pond in her backyard. On the way there, we pass a "jump-aline" as Abigail calls it, in the backyard of another neighbor, where three teens are bouncing up and down. When we get to the goldfish pond, she can't see over the fence, so she says, "soldiers"–my cue to lift her up and put her on my shoulders. From there, she can see the brightly colored "fiss" gently darting around in the water below. We enjoy the colorful site for a few moments when the pond is unsettled by what appear to be dozens of BB's pelting the surface, so we head back toward home in the rain.

Like most people, I recall precisely where and when I first heard of the attacks of 9/11. I was on Interstate 40 headed to Memphis, where I was enrolled in the MFA program in creative writing. I was still teaching full-time at a community college in Nashville, but had worked my teaching schedule around my classes. Once a week, I would make the three-hour trek from Nashville. That morning, I had a creative nonfiction workshop taught by author Randall Kenan.

My wife Clare called me on my cell phone while I was en route. Her voice was somber. "Honey, I think there is something really bad happening." She asked if I had been listening to the news. I said I had heard brief mention of a plane hitting a building in New York, but I hadn't paid much attention to the details. I pictured a small private plane catching a wing on a skyscraper and landing in the New York harbor.

After her call, I switched the radio back on and listened as the local talk show hosts tried to piece together the events as updates came in by the minute. Even at that point, I remained in a state of denial for a few more hours until the horror finally began to set in.

Clare and I spoke several more times after that. She said she had a sinking feeling that the world into which Abigail had just arrived was now changed forever. While Clare continued watching the news, she saw the second plane strike the tower, as our daughter lay there in her infant oblivion.

When I got to Memphis, several students were in the main quad of the campus standing in a circle, holding hands and praying, an uncommon sight on a state school campus, but obviously this was an uncommon morning. In class, Kenan was visibly shaken and dismissed class after a few moments. I don't remember much else that day.

Now it was three years later, and it was obvious the war in Iraq was not going to be the cake walk that running the Taliban out of Afghanistan had been (or at least was at the time). Large anti-war protests were held in San Francisco and New York and drove the schism in the country deeper. The level of rhetoric toward the president began heating up.

In the meantime, Abigail learned her colors and letters. She became a big fan of Clifford the Big Red Dog and Larry the singing cucumber from the *Veggie Tales* videos.

Depressed by the onslaught of negative new reports that spring, my wife and daughter and I went away for a weekend to the Cumberland Mountains near Crossville, Tennessee. The Cumberland Plateau has always been a place of respite for me. I love to go there for writing weekends or to just get away from the congestion and noise of Davidson County. When we arrived at the rented condo, the sun was shining and a warm breeze caressed our faces. When the tornados are not brewing, springtime in Tennessee can be glorious.

After we unpacked, Clare and I put Abigail into her stroller and took a walk to Lake Catherine, a small lake nearby where retirees have pontoon boats hooked up to docks and old men sit and fish for rainbow trout on quiet piers for hours at a time.

While we sauntered briskly down a sidewalk toward the lake, Abigail saw a skunk that had been hit by a car and was lying in a ditch. She had seen skunks in her backyard and thought they were cute, but knew not to get too close to them.

"That skunk sick?" she said with a thick lisp as she pointed. Clare and I looked at each other quietly. I knew this moment would come one day, but I wasn't quite prepared for it just yet.

"No, he's . . ." I struggled for the right words. "Well, he might be sick," I said. "But he might be . . ." I managed to change the subject for the moment, but I knew that we would have to come back this same way.

When we returned, she sat up in her stroller, straining to find the skunk. "There he is," she said. "Why he still there?"

We stopped the stroller. "Well, Abigail, sometimes people—I mean, animals—well, people too. Sometimes they get hurt really bad and they don't get better."

She stared at me as if to say, "Go on."

"They—well their body anyway, stays here, but we believe they go to another place."

Abigail looked at me quizzically. "Where they go?" she said, her voice inflecting.

This was going to be tough.

My wife looked at me with compassion. Her eyes said, *Boy I don't envy you.* "Well, sweetie, we believe there is another life after this one," I said.

"Where's that?" she queried. The girl was way too advanced for three. A litany of other questions followed. "Where people go? When they come back? Where the skunk go?"

I did my best, but explaining life and death at this stage was a little overwhelming for me. All I wanted was to eat some catfish, enjoy the scenery, sleep in for a few days, and not have to think about research papers, tenure applications, or war. I think I bluffed my way through my conversation with my daughter, but I knew this would not be the last time we would visit that topic.

Back in the real world, the attacks on U.S. soldiers increased. The beheading of Nick Berg issued in a new era of psychological warfare, one almost beyond comprehension for most of us in the West. The networks and the major dailies—the same ones who later treated us to dozens of photos of Abu Ghraib—wouldn't run photos of Berg's body, but a hideous video of the ritual found its way onto the Internet, complete with footage of Berg's screams to spare his life, and one of the Jihadists proudly displaying his head like Hamlet holding Yorick's skull.

Unfortunately, he would not be the only one. Over the next several months, others suffered the same fate, including a woman from Britain—all civilians.

The reactions were fairly predictable. The political left began to call for an immediate withdrawal. The far right wanted to turn Afghanistan and Iraq into a glass factory. The rest of us in between didn't know how to react. We wanted to do something, but didn't know what. So we stared at each other uncomfortably when the topic came up, with an uneasy, McCarthy-era-like suspicion, taking the other person's political temperature before speaking.

Some of my friends joined the protests; others began looking at survivalist websites. But in the end, most of us didn't do much of anything. We kept going to work, watched the NBA playoffs, and went to movies. We put our emotions on the back burner, somewhere behind the bratwurst, on the barbecue grill and wondered about the future. We went back to being comfortably numb.

I fell in love with the Cumberland Plateau when I first moved to Tennessee. Much less commercial than the nearby Smoky Mountains, the plateau still contains vistas and trails almost as majestic if you know where to look. As you head east on I-40 toward the plateau, your ears begin to pop as you ascend about 2,000 feet quickly. Only about a two-hour drive away, the area had become my haven, my refuge. There, nestled in

the crests of these ridges, I felt shielded from the spring tornados that were prevalent in the flatlands of west Tennessee,
and from the troubles of the world. I could exist in a reality
vacuum here, if only for a few days. Or so I thought.

Dotting the country roads on the plateau are old general stores where old men in overalls still sit and whittle and
gossip on the front stoop. Inside the stores, the thick glass
bottles of Coke are submerged in ice-cold water in old red
tanks with the paint peeling on the outside. The shelves
are filled with Moon Pies, homemade salt-water taffy, Hank
Williams Jr. ashtrays, and coffee cups with George Jones'
picture on them. On a windy road just north of Crossville is
the Alvin York Museum, dedicated to the World War I hero
who was, ironically, a conscientious objector before finally
enlisting.

When June rolled around, we went back to the Plateau
for another getaway. We returned to Lake Catherine, taking
a picnic lunch to a small beach area. On a Saturday afternoon, a light but steady wind coaxed the still waters of the
lake into small ripples and jostled a few grains of sand on the
brown beach. As we played in the chilly water, the clouds on
the horizon began turning darker. We were one of only two
families there.

The other family consisted of a mother, her husband,
and their two-year-old daughter. The mother, pregnant with
another child, sat and did needlepoint in a lounge chair
while her husband, a muscular, tanned, young man with
close-cropped hair sat near the beach on the sand, staring at

the water and writing in a journal. Their little girl built sand castles.

Abigail quickly made friends with the other girl, whose name was Alex, I believe, and the two played in the sand together, oblivious to the ever-darkening skies.

My wife and I struck up a conversation with the woman, and her husband eventually joined us. They were originally from California. He was a soldier, stationed at nearby Fort Campbell in Kentucky, home of the 101st Airborne Division. He had been in Iraq for the initial phase of the war and was on leave, but would be going back for his second tour soon. He would miss the birth of his next daughter. He wasn't sure where he was going, but thought it might be Fallujah.

Once again, the global village had closed in on us there on that small stretch of sand in the Cumberland Mountains. The conflict half a world away had again been brought to our feet, despite my best efforts to escape it.

I spoke with the soldier for a long time, but he never said whether or not he supported the war. Perhaps he thought that was a luxury he couldn't afford. He was not in a position to sit around and theorize about hypothetical scenarios on talk shows, or play Monday morning quarterback after the fact and offer up perfect solutions. Like those who had gone for two centuries before him, he would follow, trusting that he was involved in a noble cause.

I watched Abigail and Alex build sand castles together as we talked. Where he was going, the children knew a lot about RPG's and IED's and suicide bombers, but not much about

Clifford or Big Bird, or freshly mown grass, or a safe, warm place to sleep.

We talked for a few more minutes, and then they left. He had to be back at Fort Campbell the next day. Clare and I and Abigail drove back to our condo in silence. The young couple was on my mind the rest of that day. By Sunday night, he would probably be in a C-130 high over the Atlantic.

My summer classes would not begin for a few more days, so we stayed on the plateau until Monday morning. On Sunday night, Abigail fell asleep on my lap. I put her to bed, stepped outside on the patio, and stared up at the silent, star-lit Tennessee sky. I tried not to think about anything—the soldier, the war, my daughter—but it was impossible. I thought about Alex and Abigail and the world they would grow up in, and how different it would be from the one I knew when I was young. I thought about the child in the soldier's wife's womb and wondered how old she would be when her father saw her for the first time—or if he would.

As I stood there, I heard the hum of a distant engine, piecing the otherwise soundless night as it grew louder and louder. It sounded large, like a transport plane of some type. For a few moments, the sound reverberated in the dark just above us. Then just as quickly, the noise faded, getting softer and softer in the distance as the plane traveled on to its destination, on to distant lands that were getting closer and closer every day.

Somewhere to Get To

About suffering they were never wrong,
The Old Masters: how well they understood
Its human position. . .
In Breughel's Icarus, for instance:
how everything turns away
Quite leisurely from the disaster;
the ploughman may
Have heard the splash, the forsaken cry,
But for him it was not an important
failure; the sun shone
As it had to on the white legs
disappearing into the green
Water; and the expensive delicate
ship that must have seen
Something amazing, a boy falling out of the sky,
had somewhere to get to and sailed calmly on.

"Musee des Beaux Arts" by W.H. Auden

It will be a long time before I'll be able to forget Chris Pelham's face.

A photo of the then 21-year-old Gallatin, Tennessee resident appeared on the front page of the *Nashville Tennessean* on Sunday morning, April 9, 2006. His close-cropped hair showed signs of various abrasions on his forehead, along with splatters of dried blood. His blue and white athletic jersey was torn in several places and was splattered with mud. A neighbor kissed him on the forehead and tried to comfort him as he closed his eyes.

Just before the photo was taken, Pelham had checked himself out of the hospital to search for his mother, Crystal Graves, who was still missing after an F-4 tornado hit the town of Gallatin, just northeast of Nashville.

On Friday afternoon, Chris and his mother huddled together in a first-floor closet of their home after hearing on the news that they were right in the path of a killer tornado. Seconds later, they felt the house begin to shake, then the roof came off as a deafening roar filled their ears. Graves tried to hold on, but the twister tore her from the closet into the vortex of the tornado, then Chris was sucked out as well. "I was turning in the wind with the debris," he told the *Tennessean*. "We were just cotton flying."

He was found later next to the Lee Electric Building, about 100 yards from their home on Katherine Street. He had a sore back, pinched nerves, and various cuts and scrapes, but he survived.

Crystal did not. She was found the next morning, amid the debris left from the tornado about 150 yards from their home. Some papers belonging to her were later found in Bowling Green, Kentucky, 100 miles away. The last words she spoke to Chris before she was torn from him were "Chris, I love you."

The week before the tornado, I taught the W.H. Auden poem, "Musee des Beaux Arts," in my Introduction to Poetry class. Frustrated by the inability of the students to grasp the theme of the poem, especially when the anthology we were using included a picture of the Brueghel painting that inspired the poem, I skulked back to my office in the Kisber Library Building on the campus of Nashville State Community College in West Nashville. The poem's theme is about the lack of empathy we often have for those who are suffering when we don't have a close connection with them. When Icarus' wings melted and he fell from the sky, as he did in the classic mythical tale, the ploughman in the painting kept tilling the land, because, "for him, it was not an important failure," and the people on the expensive delicate ship who must have seen something, "had somewhere to get to, and sailed calmly on."

Perhaps it's a defense mechanism—we are only capable of so much pity and compassion before it causes us to be debilitated—or maybe it is just indifference. Either way, the Auden work was fresh on my mind as I tried to come to terms with the tragedies of that April.

As I read the story of Chris Pelham and his mother in the *Tennessean*, what bothered me the most was the fact that they had done everything right. They didn't try to drive in the storm. They heeded the weather reports. They had battery-powered radios in case the power went out. They went to the safest place in their house.

But it was not enough.

When the skies cleared from the three-day round of storms that hit Tennessee between April 6-8, 12 people in Gallatin were dead. Twelve others died in other locations around the state, 160 were injured, and over 3000 homes and businesses were either damaged or destroyed across a twenty-county area. The Woodhaven subdivision in Gallatin was almost completely flattened as the 200 mile-per-hour winds cut through their neighborhood like a weed whacker through a brush patch.

At our sister college, Volunteer State Community College, sections of roof were torn off and several cinder block walls flattened just moments after classes had let out. One professor hid under his desk in his office. The desk was the only thing in the room that was left when the winds finally fell silent. On Nashville Pike, a main thoroughfare through the city, several cars and a semi-truck were picked up and tossed aside like play toys.

That day, after I left class and returned to my office, I noticed the winds picking up about 2:00 p.m. and I logged on to the Weather Channel's website. As I looked at the local forecast, I noticed something unusual. The words scrolling across the site read, "This is a very dangerous storm!!!" I realized then I would probably hunker down at school until evening rather than risk trying to get to my home in Mt. Juliet—a 40 minute drive—during rush hour, when there was a good chance of tornadoes.

It was a First Friday, the day when a group of my colleagues typically meet around 4:00 p.m. at Calhoun's restaurant on White Bridge Road. I considered going to Calhoun's, but wanted to do some writing first. I loved Fridays, when the rest of the faculty would head home and the suite was quiet.

I wanted to finish an article I was writing for the *Nashville Business Journal*. I knew that if the power went off, I might not be able to get the story submitted before the deadline, which was today. I did my final edits, attached the document to an e-mail and hit 'send' just moments before the security sirens went off, signaling the approach of a tornado and warning us to go to a safe area. Luckily, the safe area for our building was just outside my office. As fellow faculty members filed in, someone brought a TV that could pick up the local TV stations with just an antenna and we all watched as the latest developments were broadcast. Most of the classes had earlier been dismissed.

The watches were elevated to warnings (meaning funnel clouds had been spotted in the area), and we stared and waited. An hour or so after that, the local weather person say that Gallatin had been hit by what appeared to be an F-3 or F-4, and that Volunteer State Community College had been damaged pretty significantly. Sections of its roof were gone and portions of several buildings were ripped away. Other portions of town had been decimated and several deaths were already confirmed.

I didn't feel much like going to Calhoun's.

Of all the forces of nature, few have captured my imagination like the tornado. The incredible force of twisters and their unpredictability, as well as how, where, and why they form in the first place, has always been a source of fascination for me. University of Chicago professor Tetsuya Fujita, along with Alan Pearson, a former director of the National Severe Storm Forecast Center, developed the Fujita scale of measuring tornadoes. Originally, the scale had 14 levels (F-0 through F-13) but later measured the storms in just six levels (F-0 through F-5.) Occasionally, a storm is given an F-6 rating, but the vast majority of tornadoes are F-1 through F-3.

The Fujita scale does not measure the intensity of the tornado itself, but the intensity of the *damage* sustained afterward. Theoretically, a tornado with wind speeds of 300 mph (normally an F-5) could pass through a town, but if it does not touch down, it might be categorized as an F-1 if it only causes minimal damage.

The F-0 level is often used to categorize storms that contain high, straight-line winds rather than actual funnel clouds and other tornadic activity. An F-1 contains winds from 73-112 miles per hour. In an F-1, sections of roofs are often pulled off homes, garages can be damaged, and mobile homes and automobiles are overturned. An F-1 is fairly easy to survive as long as you are not in a mobile home or automobile.

An F-2 is often accompanied by large hail and deadly lightning strikes. Mobile homes can be demolished, large trees are uprooted and light materials can be carried miles away. Wind speeds range from 113-157 miles per hour and a clear funnel cloud is usually visible.

In an F-3, severe damage occurs. Roofs and some walls torn off well-constructed houses; trucks and train cars can be overturned; most trees in forest uprooted; heavy cars are lifted off the ground and thrown. Wind speeds can reach up to 200 miles per hour.

In an F-4, there is devastating damage. Well-constructed houses are leveled; structures with weak foundations are blown significant distances. Cars are thrown like large missiles, and the wind speed inside the funnel cloud can range from 207-260 miles per hour. If someone is sucked into the vortex of an F-4, the winds are so intense that clothes are often sucked off the body.

In the movie *Twister*, one of the characters describes an F-5 as the "finger of God." Wind speeds can top 300 miles per hour. Not only houses, but also entire foundations can be scraped from the ground as with a buzz saw with no evidence remaining that there was even a residence. In May of 1997, in Jarrell, Texas, an entire subdivision was swept away in an F-5—along with the debris. Afterward, it was difficult to tell that a neighborhood had even existed there.

The area referred to as Tornado Alley extends from the western panhandle of Texas and includes parts of Colorado, Oklahoma, Nebraska, Iowa, and South Dakota. However, Arkansas, western Tennessee, northern Alabama, northern Mississippi, and northern Georgia are also tornado-prone areas, although the deadliest tornado in U.S. history actually occurred in the tri-state area of Illinois, Missouri, and Indiana on May 18, 1925, when 695 people perished in the 219-mile path of a twister. Tornadoes can occur as far south as Florida and as far north as Wisconsin and even Canada. Most of the tornadoes that hit Florida, however, are spawned from hurricanes that make landfall.

The tornadoes that track across Tennessee often start to break up by the time they reach middle Tennessee and move on toward the foothills of the Smoky Mountains, as the irregular terrain causes them to lose their intensity. Tornadoes favor the flat, open spaces of states like Oklahoma and Kansas. The deadliest tornado ever to hit Oklahoma was on April 9, 1947, when 185 people were killed and another thousand injured. In a typical year in the U.S., 60-70 people die as a result of tornadoes, most of them in and around Tornado Alley.

In the central U.S., tornadoes form when the warm, moist air moving north from the Gulf of Mexico meets the cool dry Canadian air that is moving southward through the Rocky Mountains. The nation's mid-section is the halfway point between the equator and the North Pole, and it is here that the battle between the competing air systems begins. The most frequent outbreaks of tornadoes are in the months of April and May. As the Jetstream moves these air masses eastward, the two forces collide. When the hot air rises and is replaced by the colder air moving in rapidly beneath it, a super cell thunderstorm is formed. If the conditions are right, the updraft of the cold air into the super cell begins to rotate, causing a funnel cloud. In many tornadoes, the funnel does not touch down and the damage is minimal.

As harrowing as these storms can be, people in some places just get used to them. In Oklahoma, baseball umpires often won't even cancel a Little League game until they spot the funnel clouds. In Arkansas, tornado parties, similar to hurricane parties they have on the Gulf Coast, are common. Storm chasers in these states actually try to get as close as they can to a tornado, to capture this phenomenal force of nature in videos and photographs. Others simply calculate the odds of a direct hit on their homes, dismiss it, and go on living their lives. For, them it's just business as usual in The Alley. I have never gotten quite so comfortable with them.

My first experience with a tornado was on April 15, 1998, ten days before my wedding. I was on my way to down-town Nashville, where I was to meet my fiancée to get our marriage license at the Davidson County Clerk's office. My fiancée Clare was waiting for me at the Howard School Building on Second Avenue, where the county clerk's offices are located, when a tornado formed on the west side of Nashville and began tracking toward downtown. I was heading in the exact same direction and was probably a mile or so ahead of it as I drove on in my state of marital-induced oblivion.

I left work that afternoon and drove toward downtown while, unbeknownst to me, two F-3 tornadoes followed me. I didn't even have the radio on, which was unusual for me, or I would have heard the weather reports.

I exited the interstate and drove across the James Robertson Parkway Bridge. I was now heading westbound and saw for the first time the black mass that had been in my rear view mirror the entire trip. It didn't look like a tornado. This one was more like a large blob, like the ones that swallowed cities in old B-movies.

I crossed the bridge and was nearly in the vortex by the time I realized what it was. I noticed what appeared to be bolts of lightning flashing in the midst of it. I later realized that the flashes were transformers popping. Then, for the first time, I saw the rotation in the black cloud as it enveloped the skyline. I saw windows blowing out of the state government buildings and people running for cover.

I was a few hundred yards from the tornado and knew it was too late to turn around and try to outrun it, so I tried to beat it to the other side of the bridge. Just as I pulled into the Davidson County Courthouse parking lot, I saw what I thought were more bits of glass falling from the skyscrapers. Again, I was mistaken and realized later they were chunks of golf-ball sized hail. I pulled into a parking space, got out quickly, and raced toward the courthouse, knowing that the granite and steel structure would provide safety.

As I ran toward the building, the 100 mile-per-hour winds pushed me back. I couldn't move. It was like a dream where I kept running but couldn't go anywhere. I was literally running in place. I could see the door of the courthouse and saw someone motioning to me as the deafening roar of the wind silenced what he was shouting. I turned to my left as debris began to blow in my eyes and I saw a homeless man being lifted horizontally by the wind as he held on to a parking meter. I thought I might not be getting married after all.

The people in the doorway of the courthouse tried to close the large iron door against the force of the wind and motioned for me to hurry. I stooped to keep myself from getting swept away by the winds. When I was about 10 yards away, the wind let up for just a second or two, and I raced for the doorway and jumped in as they closed the doors behind me.

Seconds later, the power went off in the courthouse and we were enveloped in darkness. But we were safe. The people working on the upper floors were moving to the basement to keep away from the flying pieces of glass and I followed. Some had Bic lighters and held them up for us to see when the lights went out. We waited there for about a half an hour until we got word that it had passed.

A thought flashed through my mind. *Where was Clare?*

I knew she had a habit of running late, so there was hope that she might not even be downtown yet. *Oh, God, please don't let her be in the middle of all this*, I thought.

Later, I found out that she had made it to the Howard School Building. When the sirens went off, they herded the state workers into the storm shelters and she stayed there for at least an hour, only to emerge to see the devastation wrought by that tornado as it cut a swathe across downtown Nashville and across the suburbs of Donelson and Hermitage. I found out later that evening she was OK. It was one of the most horrifying days of my life, and my first close encounter with the awesome power of nature.

As a Christian who believes in free will, I can understand violence. We are free to either love each other or kill each other, I also realize that we cannot suspend natural laws and the laws of physics and accidents sometimes happen. But the things that challenge my faith more than anything are natural disasters. I fail to understand their place in creation.

I read Viktor Frankl's *Man's Search for Meaning* in my freshman philosophy class at Walsh College in Ohio. A victim of the Nazi Holocaust, Frankl felt that he was able to survive when others simply gave up because he had established in his mind that there was a purpose for him being there. He later wrote that, by sharing his experience, he would serve humanity by making us more compassionate people, more attuned to the suffering of others. I understand that we can take these experiences and grow from them, learn from them, or allow them to make us more compassionate. But why do they have to happen in the first place?

Amy Hawkins was in the path of the band of tornadoes that ripped through Gallatin in 2006. Her two small sons were with her in their Hendersonville, Tennessee home when they heard the warnings. Her husband, Jerrod, was at work in Brentwood, where he worked as a firefighter.

When the sirens went off, Amy huddled in a closet with her two boys. When she realized the storm was about to tear her roof off as well, she threw herself over them to protect them from the falling debris. All three survived, but Amy's act of heroism cost her the use of her legs. When large sections of a brick wall fell on her, she was paralyzed from the waist down.

The community in Hendersonville responded quickly. In addition to their outpouring of sympathy, personal and financial assistance, the community started a petition to convince the producers of the cable television series, *Extreme Home Makeover*, to build Amy and her family a new home. A year after the tornado, the producers of the show chose to build Amy a new home, complete with all of the state-of-the art amenities for the disabled. Hundreds of people from the community assisted, including many Nashville country music artists like the Oak Ridge Boys and Hank Williams, Jr. She now has a swimming pool with an electronic lift to lower her into the pool so she can swim with her children.

Perhaps this was the type of redemption Frankl was referring to, how our common humanity and compassion unite us, if only for a short time.

This capacity of humans to rebound, and rebuild their lives after such a catastrophe has always amazed me. Within a year of the 2006 storms, most of the homes and businesses in Gallatin were rebuilt. The damages at Volunteer State were repaired and classes resumed. Students graduated. People moved on.

I did eventually make it to Calhoun's that evening, and my colleagues and I spent the next several hours watching the continuous news coverage of the event. By 8 p.m., we all headed home. Final exams were coming up, and I had several other freelance projects to begin work on. There were cars to be fixed and yards to be weeded.

For now, I can still vividly recall huddling in the restaurant with my colleagues that evening, April 7, 2006, and watching the weather events as they unfolded in the nearby suburbs. But I had "somewhere to get to," and had to move on with my life. I knew over time, the details would begin to fade, and at some point, I would probably forget about the events of that day altogether.

But I doubt that Chris Pelham will be able to do the same.

Brochures From Hawaii

Around December, they would usually come. Thick, oversized envelopes with extra postage stuffed in the mailbox along with Christmas catalogs, junk mail, and the ever-present stack of bills. When my mother would finally sit down to look at them, she seemed genuinely happy, a state I seldom witnessed in her. As a boy, I believed there must have been magic in those envelopes: some transforming power that could somehow lift my mother out of the color-less gray of a northern winter, and plant her in the middle of a Technicolor tropical paradise, if only for a moment.

Winter nights are long in northeastern Ohio. Sometimes as early as October, the first white flakes began to appear and drift softly to the hard earth. The sidewalks then disappear under the coal dust-encrusted snow, from the soot of the nearby power plant in Stratton, and sometimes do not reappear until April. I can still remember the strange sensation of taking off my winter boots for the first time in several months, sometime in April and feeling the hard pavement under my feet. In the fall, after the time change, the cold is compounded by the early dark, which creeps in as early as 4:30 in the afternoon, not long after school lets out. When I was a boy, it was not unusual for my brother and me to fall asleep in front of the television before the evening news came on—sometimes even before we ate dinner—while we curled up on the couch as the draft from the whistling wind snuck under the gaps in the window pane and into the living room to whisper to us and remind us that we were only a few feet, and sometimes only one electric payment, away from the mercy of the elements.

On the hillside above Route 7 that runs through Wellsville, icicles would form and grow by a few drops each day until they became mighty stalactites that eventually broke off and tumbled onto the highway below, sometimes barely missing the passing motorists.

Even the spring and fall days in that area of the country could be dreary, so winter days were particularly so. I once read that the nearby Ravenna army arsenal was assigned its location during World War II because northeast Ohio had the greatest number of cloudy days per year. Long before laser-guided missiles and infrared spectrometry, bombers would drop their missiles based on visual approximations of targets. The cloud cover gave the arsenal a natural shield from the Axis forces if they ever tried to attack it. In three of the four seasons, the sky seemed a perpetual gray, the kind of weather that breeds dreaming.

The Christmas season, despite its messages of joy, peace on earth, and good will toward men, never seemed to do that much to lift my mother's spirits. The true significance of the holidays always seemed misplaced, like an unlabeled gift buried under the Christmas tree. In the midst of the yuletide celebration, we three siblings could always look forward to one constant: my mother and father always had their biggest fight of the year over the type of Christmas tree to buy. Most of the time, the hustle and bustle of buying presents, preparing meals, and attending school and church functions seemed to drain my mother.

But looking at the brochures—this was different. When they came, they would sit in a stack of unopened mail on the kitchen table for several weeks, until after the holidays. The temperatures would drop to the single digits and stay there. And after the fervent activity of the holidays smoldered and died with the last ashes of the Yule logs, and the quiet flakes of January would begin to mount in waves that would drift several feet high against the garage, my mother would sit down and dream. That's when she would open her brochures.

Sometimes I would sit on her lap and look at the colorful pictures of strange and exotic places with her. There were pictures of the ocean. At the time, I had never seen an ocean, not even Lake Erie. The closest thing I had ever seen was Guilford Lake. Sometimes we would go there on Sunday afternoons and take picnic baskets filled with Lemon-lime Kool-Aid and fried chicken, and watch the sailboats on the lake and maybe take a swim. It was so big I could just barely see the other side.

But the ocean! My sister Sherry told me that it would make Guilford Lake look puny. And in the middle of the ocean there were islands with beaches that had pure white sand, not like the dirty, brown kind at Guilford Lake. I would sit there on my mother's lap, and she would show me pictures of women who wore strings of flowers around their necks, and did funny dances in funny skirts around poles that were lit on fire. There were hotels that were fifty stories high, and there were all different kinds of bright-colored fruits, some that I'd never even seen before, like mangos. My mother told me that maybe some day we'd go there. So on those nights when the wind chill was ten below, with the snow drifts piling up outside the door—on those nights we weren't in Ohio anymore. We were in some far off place, sipping fresh fruit juices and feeling the warmth of the sun on our bodies. Sometimes I'd drift off in her lap and dream with her.

My mother and her older sister Peg looked so much alike that people often mistook one for the other. Peg moved to Dayton in 1943 to work in the munitions factories. After the war, she met and married my Uncle Carey, who worked at Wright-Patterson Air Force Base. They had three children. Carey died of complications after a heart attack in 1989, and Peg died of cancer a few years later, in 1993.

One day, after they both were gone, my cousin Jean and I were talking at her house near Dayton. Dayton is roughly the halfway point between my hometown in eastern Ohio and Nashville, where I have lived most of my adult life, so her house has often served as a way station on my various sojourns back and forth.

During our conversation, I mentioned what a happy couple I thought her parents had been. Jean was silent for a moment. She took a drag on her cigarette, thought for a moment, then blurted out, "I don't know if their marriage was all that great."

Surprised and intrigued, I asked her to elaborate. She gathered her thoughts, and then replied, "My mother was always happy when she had company or was around her kids, but a lot of the time, she was sad. There was never any infidelity or abuse, but they just didn't seem all that happy as a couple most of the time."

"Interesting," I said.

"But I remember there was a man she used to know, I think his name was Don, who contacted her after dad died. I remember she always brightened up whenever he called."

"Who was he?" I queried.

She wrinkled her forehead and took another drag on her cigarette. "I don't know the whole story. I think they either dated or were really good friends when they were young, and they kept in contact over the years."

"Did your dad know him?

"I don't think so. After dad died, my mother and Don talked on the phone several times. Mom said that Don's wife had passed away a couple of years before, and she said they were going to try to get together some day."

"So did they?" I prodded.

"No, I don't think so. It wasn't long after that when mom got sick, and then she went downhill pretty fast," Jean added. "I just wonder if my parents were really meant for each other, you know?"

"Why did they get married in the first place?"

"Well, you know. Things were different then. Here she was a girl in a strange new town. Then she met dad. He treated her pretty well, so she probably figured, 'Why not?'"

When Jean said this, it triggered a memory that now made perfect sense. At that moment, I recalled a conversation I had with her parents a few years earlier, just before Peg passed. I was in my early thirties then and was contemplating marriage for the first time. I have never been divorced, but did have two engagements and several other long-term relationships go sour.

At the time of our conversation, I was dating an attractive, but very feisty and temperamental girl in Nashville. She was a Cajun who had moved to Nashville from near New Orleans. We dated for a year or so, but I didn't see a future, and I tried to break it off several times. Each time, she would tell me no, that I hadn't built a convincing enough argument for breaking up. It reminded me of the *Seinfeld* episodes where George was always trying to break up with his fiancée Susan and was met with the same argument.

When this girl decided it was time for us to tie the knot, she basically picked out a ring and told me where I could buy it. At that point, I hadn't proposed and didn't plan to.

I hadn't had many serious relationships, but something told me it wasn't supposed to happen like this when you married someone.

I started conducting informal surveys among my friends and relatives about their engagements. I was expecting to hear stories of rapturous evenings, of gazing into each other's eyes over candlelit dinners, of quiet walks in the park, of evenings spent whispering sweet nothings in each other's ears, of counting the hours during the day until they could get to talk to each other at night.

Most of them said they experienced nothing of the sort.

Many of them, it turns out, had also experienced this "marriage-by-default" syndrome. My Aunt Peg, who was still alive at that time, related a similar story when I asked her.

"How did Uncle Carey propose?" I asked her. She thought for a moment, and then shrugged her shoulders and said, "I don't really know."

"You don't know?" I was surprised that someone would forget such a monumental moment in his or her life. I was beginning to think that I had seen one too many romantic comedies growing up.

"No, I can't remember," Peg said. "He may have never actually proposed."

"Really?" I continued. "Why not?"

"Well, when you start dating, you realize that you like each other. Then after a while, people start asking you questions. Then a little while later you start saying things like 'Well if we ever get married...' Then it turns into

'When we get married...' Then one day we just looked at each other and said, 'Well, when *are* we getting married?' That's the way it went with Carey and me, so we just set a date."

Maybe I am just a hopeless romantic, but it all sounded so anticlimactic to me.

I never thought about the conversation with Aunt Peg until I had the one with Jean. Now I knew what Peg had been trying to say. Back then, marriage for many people was just a social convention, an economic arrangement, often void of passion and romance.

Jean and I both sat silently for a moment. "I don't know for sure, but I think she may have had some real feelings for this Don guy," Jean said. "But she never got to see him after dad died, as far as I know."

I wanted to hear more about Don, but it was getting late and I was tired. Jean was always a night owl, but I could never keep pace with her. I finally excused myself and headed off to bed. We never talked about it again.

Thomas Wolfe told us that we can't go home again, but we still try. And I did again recently. While I was there, I mentioned to my mother that I needed some old baby photos for my wife's scrapbook. My mother's health had begun to fail and, as a result, she was getting out less and less. As we sat drinking coffee, we started rummaging through some old photo albums.

As I sorted through them, I noticed a particularly old one. Its pages were yellowed, and they were beginning to tear away from the binding. The backing had also lost its adhesive and the photos were dropping out all over the floor as my mother handed it to me.

Inside the photo albums was another envelope that fell to the floor. I reached down to pick it up. It was a yellowed envelope with bunch of brochures inside.

I slowly opened one of the brochures and looked at the pictures inside. As I did so, I looked at my mother. I thought of the conversations I had with her when I was younger, and the ones I had with my Aunt Peg. That night, my heart broke for my mother and her sister, and the seemingly unfulfilled lives they had. I smiled at her compassionately, and we looked at the brochures together and chatted about the memories they evoked.

After a while, I got tired and went to bed. My mother had fallen asleep sitting up in her chair as she often did. I thought about the brochures she had kept in that photo album all those years, and how they seemed to symbolize a mythical place she had never gotten to see, and a life that had not turned out the way she wanted. Then I thought about my life and my future, and I wondered what my brochures would one day look like.

HOLY CARDS

Sitting on the corner of my office desk is a pile of various pastel-colored, no-occasion cards. They are blank except for pithy sayings at the top of each one, things like: "In the face of human misery, our priorities change," or "If we are ever to love a butterfly, we must care for a few caterpillars." They have matching envelopes to go with them. I came across them while cleaning out my office recently and nearly discarded them as trash. I'm glad I didn't because I now realize they are more than just colored pieces of paper. They were given to me several years ago by an old acquaintance and are, at least in my mind, a sacred symbol of his extraordinary life.

I have a picture in an old photo album, taken in the fall of 1978. It is a photo of three young men, arms entwined, forming a semi-circle around a shorter, older man, who stands in the middle. He is almost bald, with only a few wisps of hair above his ears, and is wearing a white turtleneck and a grey jacket. He is perhaps in his mid-50s, and stands no more than 5'4". He is a simple man who has never owned a thing besides his small closet of clothes, and a modest library of books. But on the night this photo was taken, he is positively beaming.

It is a cool August night and the three young men in the photo are Tony Orohoski, my college roommate; Mike Baranack, a mutual friend of ours; and me. We are attending freshman orientation at Walsh College in Canton, Ohio. We are ecstatic at the idea of being away from home and living on our own for the first time. The nervousness and anxiety we all must have felt seems to have been overshadowed by the anticipation of what lay ahead in this next phase of our lives. It is one of those rare seasons in life when our choices seem endless.

Walsh College (now University) is a small, Catholic, liberal arts college, founded and run by the Maine-based Brothers of Christian Instruction. The men who enter this order are not ordained priests, and as such, do not say mass or give communion. They do take vows of poverty and celibacy like traditional priests; unlike priests, however, they have dedicated their lives to teaching and learning and to the church. The instructors I had there were, and still are, some of the most brilliant men I have met, schooled in the classics, true Renaissance men. Nearly all—regardless of discipline—were well read in church doctrine, English literature, Greek and Roman philosophy, and apologetics. Most had read the complete works of Aquinas, Thomas Moore, Augustine, Milton, C.S. Lewis, and many other great writers and thinkers. Many were bilingual, and several trilingual.

One of the men who answered the call to serve in this brotherhood was a Burlington, Vermont native named Charles St. James. Charlie was a descendant of the French and Arcadian immigrants who settled in the American northeast and Canada, many of them eventually migrating to the Gulf Coast, where they formed the 'Cajun population of Louisiana. Charles studied at La Mennais College in Alfred, Maine, and began his teaching career at Fall River High School in Massachusetts.

In 1960, several members of the Brothers of Christian Instruction stood in an alfalfa field at the corner of Easton and Market Streets in North Canton, Ohio and prayed about building a college there. Those fields that surrounded Walsh have since become retail strip malls, restaurants, and city parks.

Charles left Fall River High and came to Walsh in 1970. When I met him that weekend of freshman orientation in '78, I had no idea it would be the beginning a quarter century-long friendship. Charlie left Walsh for Loyola later, but continued to visit Walsh on a regular basis and returned there full-time in 1992, where he served as a counselor for the duration of his career.

The summer following my sophomore year, I took a job at Walsh working in the maintenance department. Charlie was living on campus that summer. In June, I got a call from my mother with the news that she and my father had separated.

I was devastated, but had no car on campus and could not go home. My father moved out of the house he shared with my mother, and I had no way to contact him. My mother has never had a driver's license, so she was not able to come and get me.

That night, I went to talk to Brother Charlie at La Mennais Hall, the Brothers' residence, seeking a sympathetic ear. Charlie listened patiently to me relating the history of my parents' rocky marriage. It felt strange airing my family's dirty laundry with a member of the faculty. It wasn't something I was used to, but I knew it helped. After all, he was a counselor.

When I was finished, he looked at me and said, "Well, when do you want to go home?"

"Well, I don't really have a ride," I said.

"You need to be home. I'll take you in the morning," he said.

"Charlie, it's almost a two-hour drive," I said. That's four or five hours out of your Saturday," I said. "I can't ask you to do that."

"You didn't," he said, then rose and patted me on the shoulder. "I'll see you in the morning."

The next morning, we made small talk as we wound our way along Route 30 from Canton toward the tiny Ohio River town of Wellsville. I called my mother collect—this was still in the days of pay phones—to tell her I had a ride home, and she offered to fix lunch for us.

When we arrived, I could tell she, too, was uncomfortable when Charlie asked about the big blowup. He believed in relating honestly to people and accepting them as they were, but it was hard to gloss over things with Charlie, too. He asked my mother if he could pray for us. To my knowledge, no one had ever done that before in our home.

Then he left.

Charlie was famous for keeping a notebook with the addresses of hundreds of former students. I was fortunate enough to be one of those students. Rarely did a birthday or major holiday go by that Charlie didn't send something: a note scribbled on a scrap sheet, a birthday wish, or one of his little pastel-colored cards. I can't imagine the number of hours he must have spent writing these handwritten notes of inspiration and encouragement to former students. Of course, we were the only real family he had.

I hate to admit it, but there were times when I probably didn't appreciate the effort Charlie put into these cards. Sometimes I wouldn't hear from him for a year or two at a stretch, but then, just when I thought he had forgotten about me, one would arrive in the mail, the name and address handwritten on the outside in his unmistakable tiny cursive handwriting. When the return zip code was 44720, I knew it was from Charlie.

I had been living in Nashville for about fifteen years when I got a phone call out of the blue from Charlie. It was 1998. I had just gotten married and moved into my first home. When I heard his voice mail message, I knew the voice but he sounded weak, like he was winded, or had just been out for a long walk.

He said he was planning a trip to Nashville. "There is someone in Nashville interested in joining the brotherhood, and I'm coming to see him. I'll be arriving Thursday afternoon and staying overnight," he said. "And I'd love to see you while I'm there."

When I called him back, he had that same tired sound in his voice. When I asked if anything was wrong, he said, "I was diagnosed with Parkinson's." Then he quickly added, "But I'm on some new medications that make it very controllable. I have some good days and some bad days. Today is not one of the good ones, though."

I invited him to stay at our house when he arrived, and he accepted. "That might be nice to have someone there in case I have trouble walking," he said. "If I stay with you, though, I may need some transportation from your house to go visit this young man."

I told him I'd be happy to chauffeur him around, and then take him back to the airport. "Fridays are my light days at school," I went on. "I usually just have office hours anyway," I told him. "I'll take a personal day."

When I saw Charlie getting off the plane Thursday evening, I could tell he was different. He tried to stay upbeat, but his speech was often slurred and he lost his balance easily. I took him to our house in the White's Creek area northwest of Nashville, where my wife made us dinner.

We made small talk, but eventually got around to talking about his passion: the Brotherhood. "We're in crisis, just like the priesthood. I don't know what we're going to do about the shortage of men entering the ministry," he said as he took another long breath. "I don't know what the college will do." After a long pause, he said, "The Brotherhood …it means everything to me."

"I know Charlie," I said.

I asked him if he thought the order would ever allow its members to marry, like the Episcopal Church had chosen to do. "I don't think that will happen," he said, but didn't offer an opinion as to whether he thought that would be a good thing or not. "So I want to make sure that everyone who expresses an interest knows how desperately we need them," he added. "That's why I'm here."

We talked a little longer, then he said he was ready for bed. I had to help him out of his chair. I could tell he felt awkward about the loss of his motor skills.

The next day I dropped him off at the young man's house and picked him up an hour or so later. "I still have a little time," he said. "Why don't you give me a quick tour of Nashville and then let me buy you dinner?" he asked.

After we drove around downtown for a while, we went to the Broadway Bistro restaurant near Music Row for dinner. It was a beautiful, warm night, so we sat outside. Charlie hit it off with our waiter and got his life story. He began telling us how he was starting a technology company during the day.

He told us how the Internet was going to change the music industry and talked about downloading and podcasting and all sorts of terms that I was only vaguely familiar with. After all, it was 1998.

When we got up to leave, Charlie gave the man his card and told him to keep in touch. He said he wanted to know how his venture was turning out.

After that, whenever Charlie would call, he would say that he just gotten a letter from the waiter, whose name was Kelly, as I recall, and asked if I had been back to see him. I'm sure by now Kelly is an Internet billionaire, and I'm sure Charlie continued to write to him.

Over the years, I talked with Charlie once a year or so. In the summer of 2006, I was in Ohio again for a visit. Something was urging me to call Charlie. When I called the college, the operator told me Charlie wasn't there anymore. She hesitated and I got a sinking feeling until she added, "He's living in Louisville (Ohio) in a convalescent home for the time being. I think he had a fall recently and he may be getting some therapy." Relieved, I asked for the number and she gave it to me.

I called St. Joseph's and asked for him. He sounded a little groggy when he picked up the phone, but also happy to hear from me. "When are you coming to see me?" he asked.

"How about tomorrow?" I asked.

"That sounds great," he said in a soft voice. "The food here stinks."

The next day, I arose early and made the hour and a half drive from my hometown to Louisville (there they pronounce it 'Lewis-ville.')

I snaked my way through northeastern Ohio, passing the cornfields and dairy farms along Route 39, the on to Route 30 to East Canton, where I picked up Route 43 toward Louisville. It couldn't have been a better day for a drive. The sun beamed down as I opened the sunroof of my Toyota Camry and tuned in to WQKS in Salem, listening to the whine of the steel guitars as the singers on the country station sang about lost love, cheatin', momma, and supporting the troops.

While I was driving along, I thought of the time 26 years earlier when Charlie had brought me home from college along this same route. I tried to make out the scribbled directions that Charlie had given me as I got closer. Despite a missed turn or two, I eventually found St. Joseph's and pulled past the white statues of the patron saint and into the parking lot.

Charlie was there, sitting on a bench outside the center, leaning against a walker, waiting for me. I pulled up, popped my trunk lid, and got out. He opened his arms and gave me a feeble hug. A lot of his strength was gone, but his spirit hadn't changed. No matter how long it was between visits with Charlie, it never seemed that way. He was always the same, always glad to see me, always upbeat, despite the obvious advance of the Parkinson's.

We went to lunch at a little place in downtown Louisville. I let him out and helped him with his walker, then went to park the car. When I came into the restaurant, he had already made friends with the servers and hostess. "Are you with Charlie?" the hostess asked as I entered.

"You come here often?" I laughed as I sat down.

He shook his head. "Never been here before," he said, smiling, as he picked up his menu.

We chatted about my family, about sports, about the progression of the Parkinson's. He said he still had some good days, but the bad ones were getting more severe. "The medication is working as well as it can," he said, "but it is progressive."

We reminisced a little more about Walsh. He asked about Bryan, another old roommate from college, who was then living in Nashville also. We talked about the Brotherhood and the future of Walsh. "I didn't mind it when they started graduate programs and became a 'university.' But the worse thing they ever did was get a football team here," Charlie said. "That changed the whole atmosphere if you ask me. Now instead of students serious about learning, we've got all these big jocks running around who are only there to play ball," he said, as he shook his head.

It seemed that Charlie was standing idly by, watching the things in his life that he held dear morphing into strange new creations he no longer recognized: the college, Canton, the Brotherhood, his own health—and he wasn't sure how to deal with it.

Despite his protestations, I paid the check and we went back to St. Joseph's. As I helped him along with his walker toward the front door, I could see his countenance change. "I hate this place," he said. "Everyone is just sitting around waiting to die."

When we got to his room, we visited a little longer. I could tell that Charlie didn't want me to leave.

Finally, he said, "Here, I want you to take these," and handed me a stack of cards and matching envelopes. "Put them to good use."

At first, I thought this was a hint that I needed to write to him more often. Now I realize it was more than that. "OK," I said finally.

He got his walker and walked with me to the door. "I'll call you in a few weeks," I said. Charlie smiled, and we embraced.

It was the last time I ever saw him.

The summer of 2007, I was in Ohio once again for my annual Fourth of July visit. It was hard to be in a festive mood, though. While there, my wife found out that her best friend had lost her mother. Clare wanted to attend the funeral, so I took her to the Cleveland airport and she caught a flight to St. Louis.

On the way back from dropping my wife off, I decided to take a spin past the old college. As I drove through North Canton toward the Walsh campus, I thought of Charlie and wondered if he had ever been released from St. Joseph's. I pulled in the parking lot of the college and went to La Mennais Hall. On the way in, I saw one of the few remaining faculty from my days at Walsh.

I asked him about Brother Charlie and he turned silent for a moment. "We lost Charlie last fall," he said quietly. "He wished to be buried back in Maine, but we said a mass for him here," he said. "There was a tremendous outpouring of support, from all over. We must have gotten sympathy cards from every state and a number of other countries," he said.

Cards, I thought. *How ironic.* Now it was his turn to get them. Then I remembered the stack he had given me the previous summer, and it made sense.

Charlie has been gone for several years now. As with many of my relationships, I wish I would've called him or written more often. The stack of cards still sits on my desk. Since I found them, they have served as a kind of shrine to his memory, but I know that's not what he wanted me to do with them.

I now realize that Charlie must have sensed something when we last met at St. Joseph's. He must have been asking me to carry on his legacy of encouragement. It's a little out of my comfort zone to send cards to people. I've always been more the type to just pick up a phone and call, or visit someone in person.

But the longer they sit on my desk, the louder I hear his voice, saying the final words I ever heard him speak: "Take these. Put them to good use."

Could it be Christ?

The first time I saw Lyle Crist, it was on a marketing brochure for Mount Union College. It was 1978. I knew the college must have hired a professional model for this picture because no real person could have so perfectly fit the stereotypical image of a college English professor.

In the photo, he was sitting in a dark corner of the college library, a light beam streaming through the skylight above, as he stared out the window and contemplated some deep passage from Keats or Emerson. At the time, he was starting to bald, but had grown a distinguished white beard about six inches long—the perfect length for stroking while in deep thought, but not so long that it would get in his soup. He was at least 6'3," usually wore a tweed jacket, and often would doff a British-style tam as he strolled across campus. When he spoke with students, Professor Crist would often lower his head and peer out from behind bifocals. He had the classic face of an academician, complete with the furrows in the forehead, the quizzically raised eyebrow, and the piercing eyes that seemed to be constantly and intensely inquiring about everything.

He wrote in his memoir, *Afterwords: An English Prof's Reflections on a Campus Careers,* that he initially planned to study engineering at Purdue, but switched to English literature instead. He applied the same scientific discipline toward his teaching and writing that he would have done in engineering, and he said he never regretted his choice.

When I transferred to Mount Union in the fall of 1980 to study English, I wanted to look like, and be like, Lyle Crist when I turned 60. What a great life, I thought, to be able to read and teach the great books and writers of the English language, to be surrounded constantly by people who never get older than 22, to have three months off to write, to travel to academic conferences and take paid sabbaticals, where the only requirement was to write something interesting while you were away.

Professor Crist often team-taught the Introduction to Journalism class with Professor Charles Morford, and Crist was famous for sending his students out to cover a fictitious news event each semester. The students were made aware of it in advance, so that they would not freak out if a crazy person walked into the classroom acting strange. The mysterious classroom visitor might be an elderly person (as was the case when I took the course), or an Alliance policeman, or another faculty member. The visitor was just the first clue in the mystery, and from there, the students were sent all over campus, sometimes all over Alliance, to solve the puzzle, and then write up a news story about it for the next class–using the inverted pyramid method, of course. The mystery might involve a fictitious murder to solve, or a piece of unknown campus history to unravel. Clues were left all over town, and Crist often enlisted city councilmen, firefighters, librarians and historians around town for the students to track down and interview. It was really quite a fascinating "real world" exercise in news writing, and Crist often planned the mock event months in advance.

Crist is still remembered in Alliance for several of his other books, including *Through the Rain and Rainbow*, which was inspired by an extraordinary student of Christ's during the 1950s named Richard Kinney.

Kinney arrived at Mount Union in 1951, when Crist had just begun his teaching career. Legally blind and deaf, Kinney used what was then a popular type of glove that had a copy of the Braille alphabet, to communicate with other students and faculty, and they in turn, used it to communicate with Kinney as well.

Crist took a liking to Kinney and eventually wrote two books and a number of essays about his remarkable student. Kinney was one of the first blind students to graduate college, and later became an activist for the blind, even serving as president of the Hadley School for the Blind.

Although Kinney was perhaps the most memorable student of Crist's, he valued and esteemed all of them for their individual talents and gifts. Like many teachers, he often became frustrated when they did not exert the level of academic rigor that he felt they should—even in the 50s and

60s—and he writes honestly of those experiences as well in *Afterwords.*

One of the things that endeared me to Professor Crist was an incident that took place when I was a junior at Mount Union. I desperately wanted to take his legendary creative writing class, but that quarter there weren't enough students for the class to make. This was the conservative 1980s, when everyone was majoring in accounting, business, engineering or other "practical" majors. Knowing that I was a communications major, Crist arranged for me to take the course as an independent study and agreed to meet with me twice a week in his office, where we would have a mini-lecture and discussion. You could still do those kinds of things at a small school then, before registrars and admissions departments began getting buried under layers of academic bureaucracy. The moments spent in Dr. Crist's office made me wonder what it must be like to "read" at Oxford or Cambridge, while being "smoked at," as they refer to it, by a professor while he tutored you in his office. In my undergrad days, it was still permissible to smoke on campus and in faculty offices, and I seem to recall Professor Crist lighting up his pipe on several occasions, which never bothered me.

Before he came to Mount Union, Crist taught in the Alliance City School system. In his book, he also relates a story of a time when he was summoned from his classroom to testify before a state budget hearing in Columbus concerning funding for a new vocational wing at Alliance High School. "We were asked if we wished to give testimony," Crist writes. "A paper was thrust at me to sign. I had no better surface on which to write, so I cradled the paper in my hand and scribbled 'Lyle Crist.' We then entered a huge room with Michelangelo on the walls and 400 persons gathered to listening to the august State Board of Education, which controlled $72,000,000 that day." Crist continued, "Apparently we would have missed the whole meeting if we had arrived five minutes later, because the president, holding a piece of paper in his hand, said, 'The next to speak will be. . . will be. . . I can't make out his name, but he is the president of the Alliance city board,' the speaker continued. 'Could it be. . . could it be. . .' With all eyes in focus now, the crowd emotionally set, the president struggled again, finally asking, 'Could it be *Christ*?' Would anyone offer a rebuttal to that?"

Crist may not have been the savior of the world, but he was the savior of the Alliance publish school district that day, helping to secure $2 million for a new wing at the school.

When larger schools like nearby Kent State began attracting more students and affecting enrollment at Mount, Crist would volunteer as a recruiter, although he said it always made him feel like a telemarketer rather than a professor.

I purchased a copy of *Afterwords* during grad school, but don't recall reading much of it. After all, I was going to be an author or country music songwriter some day, not a teacher. But years later, when I had been teaching English for several years, I pulled it off the shelf, now with a renewed perspective of both the book and the man, and was amazed at how much I had in common with him, not just because of the similar views we had of the teaching profession, but also of life in general. It is a tragedy that we so seldom recognize the most influential people in our lives while they are still here and have so much to share with us.

When I moved to Nashville, I corresponded with Professor Crist regularly, to update him on my career progress, or lack thereof, and he would send me notes of encouragement and updates of his travels and other activities now that he was retired.

On one such correspondence, several years after I graduated, I shared with him the fact that my girlfriend and I had just traveled to Mexico together, as she had been named one of the top sales reps in her company, and was given a free trip for her and a guest.

His response came back: "So you traveled to Cancun?" he wrote casually. "A beautiful place," he continued. "And you went with your girlfriend? I guess I'm still an old curmudgeon in some respects, but perhaps you should consider the wisdom of such an arrangement. After all, in your letters you profess to be a Christian and I know you are," Lyle added kindly, "but there could be some consequences to such a relationship that you may not be prepared for, even at your advanced age of—what is it now? Late 20s?" He closed, "Just because we are adults doesn't necessarily mean we have acquired all the wisdom we need to make the best choices. Just something to think, about from your old prof." Then he added, "I hope you receive my comments in the spirit in which they were sent, out of genuine concern, and certainly not to inflict offense."

Until that point, I had few people in my life willing to be honest enough to share their views on such a matter. And, although I was taken aback at first, I was also somewhat flattered that a former professor would be concerned enough about my life choices to offer an opinion on them. Only Crist could have delivered such a mild rebuke without my taking offense. I knew he only wanted the best for me and the woman who would become my wife. He was right, of course. This young woman and I were not a good pair, and broke up shortly after, and only in hindsight do I realize what may have happened had I been forced into a marriage too soon.

Lyle and I continued to write each other. I would often send him clips of the first articles I published, and other entertainment and publishing news and tidbits from Nashville, and he would send me interesting stories and essays that he came across, as well as the occasional letter to the editor that he sent to the *Alliance Review.*

Lyle Crist taught, wrote, and published for the love of it, not for fame or fortune, or even for tenure. Small regional publishers or vanity presses published some of his books. Lyle didn't care. He had something to say and he was going to say it.

In addition to the Kinney books, Crist wrote and published a number of other collections of poetry, several essay collections, and other works. Most of them are still available in the college bookstore. I now have copies of all of them.

The longer I taught, the more the essays in *Afterwords* resonated with me. He also wrote of the campus unrest in the 1960s, something I couldn't have cared much about as an undergrad, and how Mount Union handled it without incident when, at about the same time, four students at Kent State were shot and killed, and 13 more wounded by National Guardsmen. There were even incidents when Crist intervened to quell what could have become tragic events like those at Kent.

In one of his poems, "Take the Stars with You," Lyle expresses his frustration with what he perceives as the lax study habits of college students: "The text had 187 short stories / and two cartons of poems / and there were more than 100 pieces / of asphalt on the floor in the room / I started counting them one day," he writes. In the body of the poem, Crist laments the fact that, rather than think critically about the stories, poems, and novels themselves, students too often simply parrot back to him the content of the lectures he has given over the course of semester. "I am afraid," he closes the poem, "that soon I shall / do no more / than count the tiles / on the floor."

I couldn't relate to the poem the first time I read it. But after 10 years or so of teaching, I saw it in an entirely new light. Crist also writes of the seminal moments in a teaching career also, the rare but nearly euphoric moments all teachers experience that make all the other frustrations pale in comparison, the moment when the light goes on in a student's mind and in her eyes, and a short story or poem hits home, and the whole purpose of a liberal arts education in a high-tech world finally clicks.

At a homecoming weekend alumni lunch in 2004, I heard that Professor Crist had been diagnosed with Alzheimer's and was going downhill quickly. My heart sunk when I heard this. I wondered if I had ever accurately conveyed to him what a role he had played in my life in so many ways: as a teacher, a writer, and a mentor and, if not, if I would ever get the chance to do so now.

He passed away less than a year later.

Everyone would love to leave behind great wealth, institutions named after us, or great works of art, but the legacy that a great teacher or mentor can leave on generations of students can be even more impactful.

Lyle Crist left that kind of legacy.

On my last trip to Mount Union, I saw that Professor Crist's books are still carried in the campus bookstore, including a history of the college that he wrote shortly before he became ill. Photos of him still dot the landscape of the college and campus center, and in dozens of college annuals, but more importantly, the seeds of inspiration that he sowed into hundreds, perhaps thousands, of students over his 50 year teaching career will have a ripple effect that will go on for decades.

A recent thread on the college's alumni Facebook site asked students to comment on memorable faculty members of their past. One student wrote of Crist, "He was a great and honorable man with a tremendous love of life." She went on to say, "With his terrible puns, his quick wit and sense of humor, every class with him was an adventure. He was a wonderful mentor and listened to your dreams. His death left a huge whole in the universe."

Would that we were all remembered that way.

HANK'S HAT

A few years ago, I was doing research for an academic journal article on the folklore surrounding the night Hank Williams, Sr. died. In the early morning hours of Jan. 1, 1953, Hank was pronounced dead at a hospital in Oak Hill, West Virginia. He was en route to a New Year's Day show in Canton, Ohio when his heart failed, largely as a result of combining painkillers with alcohol. Williams died in the back seat of a baby blue Cadillac. His driver was a 17-year-old Auburn University student, Charles Carr, who was home for the holiday break.

The trip began in Montgomery, Alabama, on December 30. Over the years, fans of Williams have sometimes rented tour busses and traveled the same path on the anniversary of the event, turning it into a huge party. In 2002, I realized it was approaching the 50th anniversary of Hank's death. I wasn't quite ambitious enough to follow the entire route from Montgomery, but I picked up Route 11 near Rutledge, Tennessee, where Hank and Carr were stopped for speeding, and followed it up to Oak Hill, talking with people and documenting many accounts of the night by locals who claim to have had a connection to Hank's last ride.

One of the many unsolved mysteries surrounding that night was what happened to the cowboy hat Williams was wearing during the trip. I would find out shortly, but only after a very circuitous route. After snooping around the Oak Hill library and talking with several of the locals who still remembered the event, I learned there was an elderly black gentleman who lived in town who might have some information to share. The librarian pointed me the way to the house, which was directly across the street from the library.

I crossed the street and walked up to the door of a large, white, Victorian home with a wide wraparound porch. A stone wall and wrought-iron gate that was locked surrounded the house. I walked around to the back, where the iron gate ended and opened into a horse barn where a man in riding chaps was combing a dark thoroughbred. "Can I help you?" he said when he saw me tentatively approaching.

"I am trying to find a William Rogers," I said. "Someone told me I could find him here."

He took his whip in hand and pointed it toward the house. "Inside," he said without looking up.

"Can I just go through the backyard here? The front gate was locked," I inquired.

"Sure, he said. "Just make sure and knock loud. He can't hear too well," he added as I headed toward the house.

I still had no idea who this man was, or what his connection might be to the night Hank Williams died. I stood on the back patio just off a kitchen door and knocked. No one responded, so I knocked a little louder. Still nothing.

After about five minutes, I started to walk back to the horse barn when I heard a voice snap, "State your business!"

"Pardon me," I said, not really sure what he was asking.

"I said, state your business!" the voice from the other side of the door barked again.

"I'm looking for William Rogers."

"Who's callin'?"

"Well, someone at the library told me that he, well . . . are you Mr. Rogers?"

"Depends."

I chuckled and continued my conversation with this silhouetted man behind the door. "Well, I'm doing some research on the night Hank Williams died and someone told me you might know something about it," I said.

I heard the deadbolt unlock and the doorknob turn. A small, old, chubby black man opened the door and smiled slightly. The booming voice that had just snapped at me through the door seemed not to fit the body I was now seeing.

"Well, come on in."

William "Raz" Rogers was then in his 90s, the grandson of a slave and the son of a miner in the West Virginia coal mines. Arthur Jones, an industrialist and captain of industry who had built the West Virginia mining industry, owned the mine his father worked in. Unbeknownst to me, I had just met Mr. Jones' son in the back yard.

I asked Raz if I could just turn on my tape recorder and ask him a few questions and he obliged. However, once the recorder was on, Raz proceeded to tell me his life story, in excruciating detail, along with a brief history of the coal mining industry, World War II, and Jim Crow days in the South. I barely got a question out once Raz started talking. I didn't find out much about the night Hank Williams died, but I found out some interesting folklore about Hank's hat.

In the Jim Crow era in which Raz grew up, he didn't have an opportunity for an education and, were it not for the elder Jones taking a liking to Rogers, he would have been destined to spend his life in the coal mines as his father did.

When Raz was just 13, he went to work in the coalmines. This was obviously before child labor laws were enacted. The elder Jones hated to see a boy working in the mines, so he offered him a job as his personal chauffer. Like the old man in Charles W. Chestnut's short story, "The Goophered Grapevine," or the old man in "The Story of the Old Ram," by Mark Twain, Raz launched into the first of a series of tales about his life that would keep me spellbound for the next 3-4 hours.

"I tol' ol' Mr. Jones that I didn't have no driver license, but he told me no matter. He'd get me a permit," said Rogers. "Long as I's with him it wouldn't matter none. So I commenced to learnin' how to drive. At first I couldn't hardly see past the steering wheel, but I growed up a little that year and then I was fine."

"So I went to work for 'im in nineteen and twenty-three, and was his chauffeur up until he died. After that, his son moved out da house and they told me to come and move in here. Said ain't nobody gonna want to rent this place anyway, and the young Joneses didn't want to stay here no mo', so they said I could look after it. They even set me up in here with a trust fund and a visitin' nurse and anything I need, I just tell young Mr. Jones and he see to it that it get done. They treat me like family."

Each time I would try to interject a question about the night Hank died, I was cut off, but the yarns were so enjoyable and fascinating to listen to that I almost forgot why I had come.

"So were you there when Hank's Cadillac pulled up in front of . . .?"

"I drove for Mr. Jones up until I got sent off to World War II. And he coulda got me out if'n I'd a wanted to, but I thought it was the right thing to do to serve my country. My momma didn't handle it too well, though. She would always write me these letters telling me how she was dying and wanted me to come home."

Raz paused for just a moment, so I thought I would give it another shot.

"Do you think Hank was really dead by the time . . ."

"My momma got remarried and she was living up in Cleveland, Ohio. She took sick and kept writing me these letters, telling me to please come home and see her before she died. And I finally wrote back and tol' her, 'Please don't send me any more a dem pitiful letters.' I said, 'I'm all the way over here on the other side of this ocean. I tol' her I can't swim across it, and I can't drink it up, so I don't want to get any more letters cause they just make me feel bad.'"

And so it went for the next three hours. I heard about Raz's life growing up in a coal mining town, about his father's life in the mines, Raz's time in the army, and his adventures driving old Mr. Jones around the state for over 40 years, along with a truncated history of Fayette County in West Virginia.

Before I left, I did manage to bring up the topic of Hank's death one more time and Raz shared some of his thoughts on that New Year's morning in 1953. "I seen they was a crowd starting to mill about over at Burdett's gas station. Dat's where they had the car. They already done took Hank to the morgue down the road to pronounce him dead and brought him back to the Tyree Funeral Home over there. I heard they was making plans to send him back to Montgomery to bury him, and they was trying to figger out who was gonna take the car back. Dat poor old college boy had to get back for classes soon. He didn't have no idea what he was gettin' into when he took that job," Raz chuckled.

"Folks was taking pictures of the Caddy," and some of 'em was millin' around in the back seat and stuff, looking for souvenirs and such. So Pete Burdette pulled it into the station bay and shut the door. That's when the hat disappeared. The hainted hat."

"The what?"

"Hainted hat," he said. "The hat Hank was wearin' that night. Somebody snatched the hat outta dat car." Raz leaned over to me and looked around as if to keep someone from hearing him, the said quietly. "Ain't nobody knows this, but it was Pete Burdette took 'at hat."

Now I was really on to a story.

"Wait a minute," I said. "Are you sayin' Pete Burdette took Hank's hat out of his car?"

"Sho 'nuff. He probably didn't see it as stealing," Raz chuckled. "He knew Hank didn't have no use for it no mo.' He figured it was a piece a history or maybe part 'a his pay for storin' the car there and all his trouble," he said.

"Go on," I said, although, by this point, I should have known, this was the wrong thing to say to Raz Rogers. He launched into another history of Oak Hill and the lineage of the Burdette family before finally circling around to answer the question about the hat.

"And I know'd that hat was hainted 'cause right after he started wearin' it, the cancer got ol' Pete.'

"He got the cancer?" I was starting to sound like Raz now.

"Brain cancer's what got 'im. Least that's what da doctors say. I think it was Hank's ghost what got 'im," Raz laughed and slapped his leg. "And you know what happened after that?

"No, what?"

"The hat sat up in a closet at Pete's house for many a year. Then somebody, might a been a relative or something, found that hat and they started wearing it, too. And you know what happened to him?"

"He got cancer, too?"

"You right as rain."

"Get out," I said. "Two people who wore that hat ended up getting the—I mean, getting cancer?" I asked skeptically.

"Tol' you it was hainted," Raz said. "Ain't nobody know'd what happened after that," Raz finished. "Somebody might 'a throwd it away, or it might still be up in somebody's closet here in Oak Hill."

I sat there in stunned silence, trying to discern whether or not it was all concocted. If Raz was right, then one of the most sought after pieces of music history memorabilia, the hat Hank Williams wore the night he died, might be in a home just yards from where we sat. Or it might be just another one of the many examples of folklore surrounding the night.

"Well, looky here, I got this nurse comin' to check on me directly," Raz said, ending our oral history lesson as quickly as he had begun it. "Pleased to know ya," he said, stretching out his hand. "You keep in touch and let me know where I might be able to read that article you writin'," he said, then escorted me down the steps and through the iron gate on the grounds of the former Jones home. I walked to my car parked on Main Street in Oak Hill, and realized I was early on the exact spot where Charles Carr had pulled over to check on Hank, then run over to Burdette's Pure Oil Station to ask for help.

Years later, I would make the acquaintance of country singer Marty Stuart, the owner of one of the most impressive collections of country music memorabilia in Nashville. I asked Marty about the hat. He informed me that he did have a hat in his collection that once belonged to Hank Williams, but it wasn't the one he was wearing when he died. To his knowledge, Marty said, that hat has never been found. I thought about relaying the Raz Rogers story, but I was concerned that maybe Marty would think I was more goophered than the hat, so I let it alone.

If Raz's story was true, there is no telling where the hat might be now. Perhaps it is still in someone's dusty attic. Or perhaps it was sold in an estate sale or garage sale for pennies to someone who has no idea of its value.

A few years ago, I thought about returning to Oak Hill and thought I would look up Raz to see if I could find out some more details about the hat, so I did a Google search for him and found an obituary from an online newspaper that indicated he has passed away a couple of years earlier. He was 96.

Over the twenty-five years that I have been actively engaged in freelance writing, one of the things I have discovered is that often times, the story you go looking for is not the story you find. But sometimes the one you find is even more interesting.

In botany, the term "processional effect" is sometimes used to describe the phenomenon that occurs when bees are searching for nectar and, while doing so, inadvertently also pollinate the flowers. The term can also be used as a metaphor for writing or other creative pursuits whereupon, while in the process of doing one thing, we unknowingly accomplish other results that may be more interesting or enlightening than the original task.

I published the story of Hank's last night in an academic journal, which I'm sure was interesting to fans of country music and of Hank Williams, too. But the story of the life and times of Raz Rogers and discovering the legend behind Hank's hat were far more compelling, and a lot more fun to hear about: a reminder to all writers that we should always be open to following any interesting detours or rabbit trails, even if they take us away from the main story. You never know where they may lead.

ALWAYS TRUST YOUR CAPE

"He's just one of those who knows that life
Is just a leap of faith
So spread your arms and hold your breath
And always trust your cape."

JIM JANOSKY, GUY AND SUSANNA CLARK, "THE CAPE"

I was attending the Southern Festival of Books in 2011 in downtown Nashville when I heard the news about Jim. My former boss, Valerie Belew, dean of the Humanities Division at Nashville State Community College, saw me sitting on a bench on Legislative Plaza and plopped down beside me. After some small talk about the festival and some former colleagues, she said something along the lines of "You were friends with Jim Janosky, right?" My stomach tightened. I know any time someone uses the past tense when referring to a person, whatever follows is not going to be good news. This time was no different.

No one really knew anything, she said, only that he had taught his courses the previous Wednesday, and on Friday morning, his wife phoned the college to say he had passed away. *How could it have happened so suddenly?* I thought.

Jim was only in his late-50s. He may not have been the picture of health, but I knew of no illnesses plaguing him, so I naturally began to consider a heart attack, accident, drug overdoses, or perhaps even suicide, although the last possibility did not fit Jim. I wouldn't find out the cause for another week.

I sat on the bench after Valerie left and pondered all those thoughts about mortality that one ponders when presented with the news about the death of a friend. In this case, there were more questions than usual.

I first met Jim Janosky when a mutual colleague, David Covington, introduced me to him. David, an instructor in the biology department, knew of my love for country and folk music and said I should meet his friend Jim, who taught horticulture and who also moonlighted as a songwriter, as nearly every other person in Nashville does. No one ever called him by his first name, though, not even close friends. Perhaps 'Jim' was just too bland.

David poked his head into my office door one afternoon "You need to meet Janosky," he said, and then walked away."

"Who's Janosky and why do I need to meet him?" I shouted down the hall.

"Because you like to write about music and he's had several songs recorded. He has one on the Top 40 right now."

"Really?" I replied. It has always intrigued me why so many songwriters in Nashville, even ones who have written several hits, still tend to keep their day jobs. Was it just the unpredictability of the industry, or did songwriting not really pay as well as some people think? Do some of them just enjoy having a day job to get them out of the house or their studios? I was always curious to know kind of money could be made from a hit song, but of course, I was too polite to ask.

A few days later, David brought 'Janosky' by my office and introduced us. We often met for lunch or for coffee to chat about and country music or screenwriting, something I later learned was another one of his passions. I discovered he had written several screenplays and had a couple of them optioned, in fact, including a screenplay originally titled *Stars.* Jim often flew out to L.A. during semester breaks, and I once asked if I could accompany him to a pitch meeting. We made plans but could never coordinate schedules.

Among Jim's catalogue of songs was one he wrote with the legendary Guy Clark and his wife Susanna called "The Cape," about not living one's life in fear. One of the lines in the song says, "He's one of those who knows that life / is just a leap of faith / so spread your arms and hold your breath / and always trust your cape." Guy Clark cut it himself, as did Kathy Mattea and others.

In 2011, just before Jim's passing, I got a chance to edit and compile a collection of stories behind 101 country songs, and I chose "The Cape" to be included in the book. Jim was kind enough to share the story behind writing "The Cape," and allow us to use it. I've reprinted it here:

Susanna Clark and I were just visiting one day and we got to talking about our childhoods and the pranks we used to play. Then we started talking about how, when we were kids, we used to really think we could fly. That led to a conversation about the amazing faith that little kids have, and how they really believe those kinds of things could happen. We had several more conversations about this and started writing down random notes and phrases and lines on the idea of childhood faith. I told her the story of a guy I used to work with up in Pennsylvania. We worked at a butcher shop together. Once, when he was a kid, he tried to be a tightrope walker. He put a rope between two beams in his barn and took the tires off his bicycle and tried to go across that tightrope on the rims of his bicycle. He got about a foot and ended up unconscious on the floor of his barn. His mother woke him up just so she could beat him! She said, "What made you think you could do this?" He said, "I just believed I could!"

A few years after the song was released, Dr. Alan Kramer used the song in a film series called *Living with Cancer* series, which focuses on cancer survivors. After the film was released, Jim received the following letter in the mail:

Dear Jim: I am the patient featured in a film about lung cancer that Dr. Alan Kramer is making in the *Living with Cancer* series. Let me add my thanks to you and Guy and Susanna for allowing us to use that wonderful song, 'The Cape' in the film. I was turned on to the song this spring by a friend who knows me very well and thought that it sounded made-to-order for me; in particular, about the leap of faith. Later, I was lucky enough to attend (the bluegrass festival) Merle Fest in North Carolina and heard Guy singing it. I was blown away by him. I was diagnosed at age 65 with Stage 4 lung cancer and given only 8-10 months to live. I never quite accepted that, though, and worked hard with my doctors. I am trying to do something to change my chances. I have been very lucky and am now a five-year survivor. That is what our film is all about: the conjunction of my hard work and luck, along with the medical world's advances in treatment and drugs. In a month, I will be celebrating my 70th birthday, my five-year survival, and life in general here in Sonoma Valley with a few hundred of my closest friends and family. My friend is going to sing his version of "The Cape" and we are going to show rough cuts of the film. Thanks again for everything. Wells Whitney.

Jim said getting that letter from Mr. Whitney and knowing his song was being used to help cancer survivors was worth far more to him than any royalty check he ever got from the publisher.

In the fall of 2010, Jim began having excruciating back pains and nothing would help. He would often curl up under his desk in between his lectures at Nashville State, because that was the only position he could be in where the pain would lessen. He tried surgery, chiropractors, pain meds, but nothing seemed to help. He told his wife Annette he didn't want to live like this. As time went on, he needed stronger and stronger drugs to deal with the pain, and soon he began to have nightmares and hallucinations as a side effect. Annette began to worry about leaving him alone.

Toward the last months of his life, his wife told me, he made peace with several strained relationships, and made sure his financial affairs were in order as far as his intellectual property rights and other issues, as he knew he would probably not be around to tend to them.

Despite his sometimes stoic, skeptical nature he spent the last few weeks of his life really opening up, though. One of the men from his church later shared that he and Jim had spent many hours together in the final weeks of his life. One evening, Jim was just lying on the couch thinking. "Jim, how can I help you?" his friend asked. "Is there anything you want or need?"

"I don't know," Jim said. "I think I just need a lot more of Jesus."

Annette wasn't sure if the medication had sent him into a deep depression or if the pain was just too much to endure. "He was an amazing man," she said at his memorial service. "Here was this guy from the country, who lived in a log cabin that he built in the hills of Tennessee, and he would somehow finagle all these meetings with Hollywood producers and directors." As she said this, her voice began to crack and a tear rolled down her cheek. She pushed her blonde bangs back and regained her composure, taking a deep breath. "He just never put any limitations on what he could do, and wanted to live life to the fullest. And he did."

She found him on a Friday. It was a glorious fall morning. The sun shone on the brilliant maples and Bradford pear trees that dotted the gently rolling hills of southern middle Tennessee. That very morning, a story in *Variety* magazine announced that *Stars,* the movie he had written, was going into production. It's tragically ironic that the film's main character is on a cross-country journey, which he plans to end by committing suicide. (Author's note: The film was later renamed *Dark Under the Stars,* and was released in Europe in the fall of 2013).

Jim left the house sometime that morning, walked to his driveway, lay down with a shotgun, and pulled the trigger. Under his head and back, he had placed a handmade blanket that had been given him by a relative. Given the nature of the way he was about to take his life, Jim almost certainly did this to make the cleanup easier for the people who would find him, but I found it so ironic that the way that the way it was positioned under him made it appear that he was wearing a cape.

When I heard about this, the lyrics to his song came flooding back to me. I thought of the many fans of the song who had found hope and comfort in the lyrics. Why couldn't Jim?

Perhaps he just found a different kind of comfort in it: that maybe even as he walked to his driveway and prepared to "slip the surly bonds of earth," and fly off to "touch the face of God," he still knew that somehow, even in death, he could always trust his cape.

MY MYTHIC JOURNEY

The fall foliage on the western ridges of the Alleghenies was the color of Fruit Loops as we snaked our way through the back roads of northwestern Pennsylvania. The October sun peered through the sunroof of our Toyota Camry as my three year-old daughter Abigail dozed off in the back seat. My wife and I had gone home to Ohio to visit my mother for a few days and, while we were there, took her to see my aunt Grace in nearby Corey, Pennsylvania.

After we had lunch with Aunt Grace, someone—I'm fairly certain it wasn't me—mentioned going shopping at the nearby Blair store outlet. I dropped the three ladies off at the door and set out for some quality time with my daughter, who was just waking from her nap.

When I pulled away from the Blair store parking lot, a flash of light caught my eye. It appeared to be the sun reflecting off a body of water nearby. I was curious and turned the car in that direction. The blacktop ended, and I realized I was on a dead-end, one-lane, gravel road that followed the path of the water. The sight of ripples cascading off the rocks was breathtaking.

I pulled over and parked. I woke Abigail, lifted her out of her car seat, and we walked toward the bank. I was struck by the speed of the current of this large creek or river, or whatever it was, as the water rushed past us, just feet away. As I stood on the bank, I felt an odd sense of déjà vu.

I held the hand of my daughter, who was now pulling me closer to the river's edge, and I told her not to get too close. All the while I kept staring at the whitecaps as the river paraded by me in all its grandeur. A collage of fragmented memories began drifting through my mind. I could picture myself here. I began to recognize the bends in the river as I walked upstream and saw a spot on the far bank that looked hauntingly familiar. *I've been here before* I thought. *But when?* I had never really believed in reincarnation, but I began to consider the possibility. To my recollection, I had never been anywhere near here. When my aunt moved to this area and became a Jehovah's Witness back in the 1960s, she cut herself off from her brothers and sisters, and for decades, the family had little contact with her. As a result, we had never visited her much until I was in my late thirties. But slowly, the fragmented images began to coalesce into a more coherent picture, as I was transported back to the summer after my ninth grade year.

Of all the years I played competitive baseball, I was only selected to play on an All-Star team once, and that happened after my freshman year of high school, following the Babe Ruth League season in northeastern Ohio. Earlier that summer, however, I let my friend Scott talk me into signing up for a canoe trip with a local church group. At the time, I was unaware that I would make the post-season All-Star team, and that the tournament would be the same week as the canoe trip. These events left me in a conundrum. Since I had paid half of the $80 fee as a deposit, (a hefty sum in 1973 dollars) and my parents had paid the other half, I would have felt too guilty to cancel and lose the money, so I began making preparations to go.

The trip was coordinated by the Covenant Presbyterian Church in Wellsville, but when it came time to leave, I discovered that it would be quite ecumenical, with a lot of young people from Methodist, Baptist, and Catholic churches around the Ohio Valley also attending.

Danny MacLean, owner of the town's biggest funeral parlor, was leading the teens from the Presbyterian Church. As the date grew closer, Scott and I received more details about the outing. We were told to purchase various kinds of outdoor gear for our outing, including pup tents, backpacks, freeze-dried food, and various other camping paraphernalia. I was under the impression we were in for an Outward Bound-style adventure of some kind. I had been in Boy Scouts all my life so I was OK with the whole camping thing, but I wasn't sure Scott was very experienced in these kinds of outdoor activities.

Scott wasn't particularly adventuresome or athletic. He was, and still is, very lanky, 6'3 and all of 130 pounds, with a head of blonde hair that was cut in the Dutch Boy-style that was popular for a brief period in the 70s. A soft-spoken studious type who loved to play Elton John songs on the piano, Scott had been a good friend of mine since we were four or five years old. He moved away when a bypass for Route 7 took his home and shaved about three blocks off our already tiny hometown. His family moved to a different school district, but continued to attend the same church so we still got to see each other regularly.

So as summer moseyed along, Scott and I prepared for our big adventure. When I saw Mr. MacLean a few weeks before out trips, I peppered him for more details. "Didn't you get a brochure?" he asked.

"I guess not," I responded.

"You boys are in for the time of your lives. We've taking a 100-mile canoe trip down the Allegheny River."

All of the memories of that week came back to me as I stood on the riverbank. I cocked my head to the side and stared into the late afternoon sky, letting the search function in my brain scan the billions of memory bits in my brain trying to make a connection. Images of young teens laughing and splashing in the water flashed through my mind in fractured pictures. Slowly they became more vivid. I realized I was in Warren, Pennsylvania. *Warren?* I thought. *The Allegheny River? That's it!* I recalled. *This was not just a creek! These were the headwaters of the Allegheny.* And I *had* been here before, not in some ethereal sense or in a past life, but in *this* life! A grin of recognition crept across my face, growing into a smile and then a full-fledged belly laugh as I realized that I wasn't crazy after all. The memory dam burst and the flood of images washed over me like the waters tumbling over the rocks on the river.

Until that moment, I had almost forgotten about the canoe trip. Staring at the bend in the river, I could almost see the ghosts of two fourteen year-olds there, paddling a steel canoe, navigating the rapids like they were playing a video game. I saw myself in the back of the canoe steering as Scott paddled in the front. Four other pairs of canoers lagged behind us in our parade down the river. The trip had been one of the most exciting and terrifying weeks of my life. It was in many ways part of an epic journey, a rite of passage into adulthood for me.

The Allegheny Reservoir and adjacent Kinzua Dam straddle the New York border in the northwest corner of Pennsylvania. The area was once a Navajo Indian Reservation and most of the towns still bear testimony to that legacy: Tionesta, Tidioute, Kinzua. The river is as much a part of local folklore here as anything. For some reason, the ghost stories surrounding the Kinzua reservoir are legion.

The mouth of the Allegheny runs fresh and clear, with mountains springs serving as tributaries to the waterway. As it heads south toward Pittsburgh, the river gains volume and speed as it tumbles through the western rim of the Appalachians until it joins the Monongahela River at

Pittsburgh to form the Ohio River. The scene was every bit as idyllic as I remembered it being thirty years earlier.

The summer of 1973, I had my best season ever in baseball. I played for a team sponsored by the Patterson Foundry in East Liverpool. I had hits in nearly every game and even hit for the circuit once: a single, double, triple, and home run (albeit inside the park) in one game. For these accomplishments, I was offered a spot on the post-season All-Star team. When I realized the canoe trip was the same week as the All-Star tournament, I was devastated.

On one hand, I realized I might never get a chance to participate on an All-Star team again. Many boys in junior high get a large chunk of their self-esteem from their athletic prowess, and this was one of the few times in my life that my proficiency in any sport had been recognized.

After much agonizing, I decided to go on the trip. I packed according to the flyer we received. I took plenty of rain gear–ponchos, rain hat, galoshes–along with several sets of jeans, T-shirt, tennis shores, and shorts. I packed all my toiletries except shampoo, for some reason. I was too embarrassed to ask anyone to borrow some during the trip, and I remember my hair being dripping with grease by the end of the week. The first time I shampooed it afterward though, it felt like silk.

We left on a Saturday. We all converged on a spot near Wellsville where a half dozen vehicles carrying the unsuspecting teens met and formed a convoy before heading north on Route 11 to Youngstown, then on to I-80, which took us into Pennsylvania. For some reason, I remember listening to Billy "Crash" Craddock's "Rub It In," on the radio as Scott and I sat in the back seat, holding our noses and singing along, laughing and poking fun at Craddock's nasal vocal style.

We stopped at a canoe livery a few miles from the Allegheny Reservoir, and the truck followed us to our put-in point on the New York side of the Reservoir. We unloaded our gear and the six canoes were placed into the water. The canoe transport pulled away, as did Mrs. MacLean, who was heading back to Wellsville for the next week. As they did, I looked up at the sky to see some dark clouds moving in and got a sinking feeling in my stomach. Today when I think of that moment, it reminds me of a scene in one of my favorite movies, *City Slickers*, when actor Bruno Kirby has a similar revelation during his own mythic journey. When their cattle drive leader, Curly, has a heart attack and dies, his two not-so-noble sidekicks decide to leave the tenderfoots out in the wild with a herd of cattle. "This is no game now," says Kirby. "That other macho stuff we've been doing is all bullshit, but this is for real!"

I looked down at our bags of dehydrated food, then at our gear and tents, and then at the vast expanse of water in front of me. "What the hell have we gotten ourselves into?" I asked Scott. "I don't know but I think we're screwed," he replied as Mrs. MacLean's taillights faded into the darkness.

We set up camp on the banks of the Reservoir, aiming to get an early start in the morning. I had no idea at the time that Danny planned to cover about 20 miles a day come hell or high water. He didn't leave room in the schedule for any lag time, and the canoe truck and the other vans had been instructed to pick us up at a certain point the next Saturday and we had to be there. I would be sharing a tent with Scott for the entire trip but we would alternate canoe pairings in order to get to know each other better and establish a sense of "community."

As soon as we had our tents set up along the Reservoir, I felt the first pellets of rain dropping on our heads. "Well, I guess we should just head inside our tents and …" I started to remark when one of the other campers interrupted. "Oh no, you don't. We all have our duties for dinner and if we all don't contribute, none of us can eat."

Two hours later, we finally headed back into our tents drenched. I felt like a sponge. Not only were my shirt and jeans now dripping into my tennis shoes, but our tent had begun to leak and the backpack of clean dry clothes I had for the week ahead was now also beginning to get soggy in the midst of the monsoon-style downpour. As I laid my head on my damp pillow and tried to get some rest for the day ahead, I looked at Scott and said, "This was your idea, wasn't it?"

The Allegheny Reservoir is 24.2 miles long, from the northern tip along the New York border to the southern tip at the

Kinzua Dam. As a result, we wouldn't be getting much past the Kinzua Dam the first full day.

The sun broke through the clouds on Sunday morning as we held a campfire church service in the morning and cooked breakfast while the fog lifted off the Allegheny Reservoir. We loaded up the canoes and began our first day's journey. It was easy to see why this area was filled with so much folklore about the Native Americans. I could almost feel their spirits in the densely wooded forest that pushed right up to the shoreline. The canoe left its gentle wake behind us as we traversed our way down the narrow Reservoir. The only sound I could hear was an occasional loon or the paddle breaking the surface of the water as the others rowed on ahead. I could tell that even with a season of baseball behind me, my arms would need to be whipped into shape to make the entire trip. I knew that by the third day, they would be in shape one way or another.

The serenity and solitude that I experienced that morning and afternoon as we drifted along the waterway was one of the most pleasant experiences of my childhood. Unfortunately, the day was to end differently.

We stopped for lunch about fifteen miles down the Reservoir. All of the canoes tied onto one another, and some ate their lunches in the boats. Some others hung out on shore or, like myself, went into the woods to explore.

When Scott and I came back out a half hour or so later, we found that the others had started without us. Apparently, I thought it would be a longer stop. We then had to race to catch up. We saw the other canoes on the water a mile or so ahead. I told Scott I would take the rear since I was better at steering than he was, and we shoved off. An hour later, the sky turned gunmetal gray and flashed of lightning could be seen in the distance. I would find out later that this was not uncommon for this area. The humidity created by the rain forest-style topography often produced strong and sudden thunderstorms. Scott and I paddled harder trying to catch up. The only thing that would be worse than being caught out on the lake in a metal canoe in a thunderstorm would be getting caught *alone* out on the lake in a metal canoe in the middle of a thunderstorm.

As we approached the end of the Reservoir, the skies continued to darken, but we hadn't seen any precipitation yet. The thunder rumbling above us, however, was most disconcerting as we tried to beat the storm.

At its south end, the Reservoir expanded into a wide bay. The last leg of the trip would require us to cross an area about a mile and a half wide before we reached the Dam. I kept calculating whether or not we should attempt to cross or just wait until the storm passed. I didn't want to fall any further behind than we already were, but I wasn't looking forward to crossing that bay in this weather either.

The winds picked up and the waves began to toss the canoe about. It was harder and harder to judge how much distance we were covering because the waves were beating us back. It almost felt as though we were standing still but I could tell the shoreline was changing so we must have been moving a little. Apparently I had forgotten to ask Danny whether or not metal canoes were susceptible to lightning strikes. My basic knowledge of science told me they probably were, but I hoped and prayed there was some law of electromagnetics of which I wasn't aware that might save us yet: like how the rubber tires of a car keep the vehicle grounded during a storm and protect it from lightning. As the bolts lit up the sky all around the lake, I prayed we wouldn't light up like a Fourth of July fireworks display.

Scott and I paddled harder and harder, the waves continuing to wash up over the sides of the canoe. If we didn't get to shore soon, it would be filled with water, and we'd have to dive in and swim. I thought I could handle it. I looked back at Scott and realized, thank God, that we had both worn our life preservers. That would help us for a while, but I wasn't certain how well these worked in rough waters.

We were probably only in the water a total of 30 minutes or so, but it felt like hours. Still, we were making progress and the storm seemed to be abating just a little. When my arms felt like they couldn't row one more stroke, I looked up again and realized we were perhaps 100 yards from shore, and the wind and waves were no longer pushing us backward. I could see the shoreline slowly getting closer. We were going to make it.

Several more similar close calls that week resulted in my having a renewed respect for the water and the wilderness, the only two things I saw that week. Alternating afternoons of peaceful, calm, warm and dry days were punctuated by rain-forest-style monsoons that we plodded on through, getting soaked to the bone, along with all of our gear, clothing, and tents, in our attempt to cover the requisite mileage for the day. By the week's end, I didn't have a single piece of dry clothing. We arrived at our pickup destination just a little north of Pittsburgh on Saturday afternoon, where Danny's wife was waiting for us. We loaded the canoes onto the trailer and headed back toward East Liverpool, where our parents would meet us.

I turned 14 years old that year, about the age when boys in many cultures undergo some type of ritual to commemorate a passage into manhood. In the heart of the Brazilian Amazon live the Satere-Mawe. To become a man in the Satere-Mawe, a boy must stick his hand in a glove woven with bullet ants and withstand their stings for over 10 minutes without making a noise. The Maasai of Kenya and Tanzania have a series of rites of passage that carry boys into manhood. Boys between the ages of 10 and 20 are brought together from all across the country. Dozens of houses are built that will serve as the place of initiation. The night before the ceremony, the boys sleep outside in the forest. At dawn, they return to the little makeshift homestead for a day of singing and dancing. They drink a mixture of milk, cow's blood, and alcohol and eat piles and piles of meat. After the festivities, boys who are of age, 12-16, are ready to be circumcised.

In 21st century American culture, the closest thing we have is registering to vote or drinking our first beer, but I began to view surviving that week on the Allegheny as my transition to manhood, my own archetypical hero's journey. What I lost from not getting my ego boosted as a result of being on the All Star team, I believe I more than made up for in this test of manhood. I had stared death in the face for the first time in my life, and had triumphed.

The next year, I gathered my courage and made a decision to transfer high schools and attend nearby Southern Local High School, where I seemed to fit in better. I made the JV basketball team and even started as a first basemen for a few games on the varsity baseball team. I switched from the industrial arts program I was enrolled in to a college prep curriculum. I started taking guitar lessons, began writing songs, and even began playing in some bands. I even got the courage to start asking girls out and began dating. In hindsight, I am not sure I would have had the confidence to attempt those things had I not conquered my fears and slayed a few dragons that week in Pennsylvania.

Standing there on the bank of the Allegheny, I watched my little girl play as the rippling waters rushed past and envisioned the ghosts of a dozen teenage canoers from three decades earlier.

Abigail was getting closer to the rushing waters again. I walked over and picked her up, and put her in her car seat. She laughed as I buckled her in and I prepared for the long drive back to Tennessee.

GREGORY

(Originally published in *Number One*, Volunteer State
Community College, Gallatin, Tennessee, Spring 2012)

In the Shreve High football stadium,
I think of Polacks nursing long beers in Tiltonsville,
And the gray faces of Negroes in the
blast furnace at Benwood,
And the ruptured night watchman of Wheeling Steel,
Dreaming of heroes.
All the proud fathers are ashamed to go home.
Their women cluck like starved pullets,
Dying for love.
Therefore,
Their sons grow suicidally beautiful
At the beginning of October,
And gallop terribly against each other's bodies.

JAMES WRIGHT, "AUTUMN COMES TO MARTIN'S FERRY, OHIO"

Life in a steel mill town can be both nurturing and brutal. For Gregory, unfortunately, it was often the latter.

I hadn't seen Gregory for about fifteen years until that evening. I was staying at my mother's house in Wellsville, Ohio when he knocked on her door. When I answered, the first thing he did was ask to borrow ten dollars. He told me it was for gas, but I knew it was probably for beer. It felt odd, since we hadn't seen each other for so long. I thought he had come by so we could catch up with each other, but he just asked for the money, and then left when I gave it to him. He said he would stop by later that night when he had more time, but he didn't.

Wellsville is a small town on the Ohio River, just south of Youngstown, built on the side of hill. Then, it was a town of mostly steel mill and pottery workers, the sons and grandsons of Eastern European and Italian immigrants. They worked hard, played hard, and drank hard each weekend at the local Sons of Italy, Knights of Columbus, the Eagles, and VFW clubs. They also loved Friday night football.

Gregory and I first became friends when our fourth grade science teacher, Mr. Watson, asked me to tutor him. Each session, I would drill Gregory on the periodic table of elements and the various forms of flora and fauna. I also discovered that one learns much more about a subject when forced to teach someone else.

Gregory was built like a bank vault. Even at nine years old, he must have weighed 150 pounds. His thick hair was piled up in the Afro style that was popular in the 1970s, and he wore thick glasses connected to a strap. He wore the same dark brown, pinstriped suit, which his mother always picked out, several days a week to school.

Gregory lived with his parents and his little brother Derek in a small, two-bedroom house with white aluminum siding and a green awning across the alley from Garfield Elementary. Their dog, a large Siberian husky, was always chained to his box in the back of the house and nearly pulled the box over each time I tried to slip past him to knock on the back door.

I went to Gregory's house two or three nights a week to help him study. His mother would sometimes invite me to eat with them. Then, if we didn't have football practice, we would head off to his bedroom for our lessons. Most of the time, we got finished without a visit from his father, Milt. Other times, we weren't so lucky.

Milt would stroll into our tutoring sessions unannounced, staggering and cursing. He usually had his shirt off, his scarred black chest and arms peppered with tattoos. Pockmarked scars dotted his face, and his nappy hair was seldom combed, one side usually higher than the other. His solid frame was evidence of the factory work he had done most of his life, but a small beer gut protruded over his belt, and Milt's boxer shorts usually stuck out in the back of his trousers.

When he walked in the room, I always held my breath. I never knew what to do when the beatings started. I remember I seldom feared for my own safety—though I'm still not sure why. Beatings were a common form of parental discipline in the tough, industrial town, but the kind Gregory received was different.

Part of me wanted to run. Part of me wanted to help my friend. Most of the time, I didn't really know what to do. I usually just turned my head to a corner, tried to be quiet, and waited for it to be over. I was nine years old.

As we sat together silent on the lower bunk in the bedroom that Gregory shared with Derek, Milt would often pace the room, muttering and stammering like a Pentecostal preacher trying to call up the spirit, raising the volume and speeding up the cadences of his soliloquy. All the while, he would rant on and on about the various deficiencies in his son's character, from his lack of athletic prowess to his poor grades. It was almost as if he were trying to convince himself of the necessity of the terrible act he was about to inflict upon his son.

I could usually feel the crescendo building and anticipate just the moment when the first blow would fall. That's when I would move out of the way and into the corner. It was usually just a shot to the arm or body. After that, Milt pranced back and forth across the room ducking and feigning punches like Mohammed Ali, telling his son to fight back. Either out of embarrassment, or fear, or possibly even pity, he never did. Even at nine, Gregory could probably have taken his old man, especially in this drunken state, but he usually just put his head down until it was over.

First, Gregory would shield his head from the often-misplaced blows that might catch the corner of his bunk bed and do more damage to his father's hand than to Gregory. Then his thick glasses might fly across the room after more punches found their mark. They seldom brought blood, though. Most of the time, the only red I saw was the color in my friend's face from having to endure an ordeal like this in front of one of his classmates.

I knew the abrasions and bruises would heal in a few days, but the words would last a lifetime.

After that, Milt usually stumbled into his bedroom and passed out. The moments following these outbursts were always silent and awkward. I knew that I was witnessing something extraordinary, like the limbs of a sapling being twisted beyond their ability to ever grow straight.

The amazing thing was that I never heard Gregory speak harshly of his dad when we were little. Perhaps he simply believed, as many kids did, that this was the way they believed they needed to raise us to be tough enough to survive in the world. Milt had a softer side when he was sober. He would sometimes take Gregory and me to Pittsburgh Pirate baseball games. Once, they had a "Father and Son" day at Three Rivers Stadium, where sons got in free with their dads, and Milt took us both. When he bought his ticket, he told the woman at the booth we were both his sons. When she looked suspicious, he simply glared at her. She gave us the tickets and told us to go in.

Gregory gave football a try, but like me, never seemed to possess the killer instinct to excel at it. Toughness and meanness were the most admired traits on the Wellsville Little League football team. One of our coaches was a brutal man who spent as much time cursing us, kicking us in the pants (literally), and abusing us in every other way he could think of, as he did teaching us to block and tackle. This was before political correctness, and before the era when everyone started getting a trophy just for participating. Perhaps he thought he was preparing us for life, and in some ways, maybe he did. But I hated him for the way he treated us, and especially the abuse he heaped upon Gregory.

I still do.

We went nearly ten years without losing a game, but the accolades hardly justified the permanent scars that were left on many a young man.

The kids at school often picked on Gregory, even though he was often much larger than them. He never fought back. Perhaps it's because he knew deep inside that if he ever lost control, like Lenny in *Of Mice and Men*, or John Coffee in *The Green Mile*, he might crush them with his bare hands.

On the basketball court, though, he was a different person. He had a jump shot that hit nothing but net most of the time, even from 30 feet or more. He blocked shots like Dennis Rodman. We often played one-on-one during the summer months from the early morning hours until the hot summer sun faded over the Ohio River. I seldom won.

When we got to high school, Gregory continued to excel at basketball. He played forward for the high school team that went 14-4 and advanced several rounds into the state playoffs before losing. It was one of the few highlights in his life. Apparently, this brush with significance wasn't enough to erase the experiences of his youth, though.

After high school, Gregory worked at a series of manual labor jobs, and then landed a job at the Edison power plant down the river in Stratton, Ohio. He later ended up on disability, probably due to his increasing substance abuse. I left Wellsville in 1978 for nearby Mount Union College in Alliance. After graduation, I moved to Tennessee and seldom saw him again.

A year or so after the exchange at my mother's house, I ran into him one more time in Wellsville. My wife Clare and I were there together one weekend. We had gone for a walk around Hammond Park, a small baseball park and playground area just outside of town. While we were making our rounds, I thought I heard my name being called by someone under one of the nearby picnic shelters.

As I approached, I could see Gregory and some other guys I knew from high school, sitting on top of a picnic table, mixing sloe gin and coke. He had really ballooned up by now, probably topping 300 pounds. As I walked up to him, he grabbed me and hugged me, nearly suffocating me in the process. I introduced Gregory and the other guys to Clare.

We made small talk for a few moments. Then he asked if I could spot him a few more dollars. I said sure.

I asked him about Milt. Gregory got quiet.

"He's dead," he finally said softly. There wasn't much remorse in his voice.

"Oh. I'm sorry," I said. "When . . .?"

"About a year ago," he said. "He was coming through an alley. Ran right through something. Shattered the windshield and killed him."

"I'm really sorry, Greg," I said.

"Well, you remember what he could be like," he added, suddenly turning somber, as though he recalled the days in his bedroom. "You more than anybody."

"Yeah," I agreed. I looked down at the bottle of sloe gin. "You know Greg, if you ever need help or want to go to church or something with me . . ."

He held up his hand. He knew what I was going to say and wasn't really interested. "Oh, my mom's already tried all of that," he said.

I took a seat on the picnic table beside him. "Oh, so your mom's still around?" I asked.

"Yeah," Gregory said, offering up some comic relief to a tense moment "One day, she told me she was takin' me to a new church," he laughed. "We kept driving and driving. Finally, I said, 'Momma, where you takin' me? They ain't no churches out here.' Then she finally stopped the car and got out. It was a rehab joint!"

His laughter was infectious. I couldn't help but start chuckling, too. "What did you do?" I asked.

"I had to stay there. Didn't have no way back," Gregory said. He was howling now, rocking back and forth, hooting like an owl, and slapping me on the leg. "My own momma kidnapped me. You believe that shit?"

The other guys with him obviously knew the story and began laughing, too. So did Clare. It was good to hear him laugh, even if it was laughter born of such pain. I couldn't remember the last time I heard that sound coming from him.

We talked a few more minutes. Then I said, "Well, we'd better get back to my mom's. She's watching our daughter for us," I said. He nodded and grabbed me one more time. My wife and I then finished our walk.

As we got closer to our car, we could hear all three of them under the pavilion, still laughing, as Gregory's voice faded in the distance, "Can you believe that shit? My own momma. . ."

STALKING NELLE

When Fred Kelley walks down the street of his hometown of Monroeville, Alabama, the townspeople often call his name and wave. Fred works as a sales rep for a natural gas company in Monroeville, but he is known around town for hosting a popular talk show and oldies program, "The Phil and Fred Show," on the local 5,000-watt radio station, WMFC-AM, broadcast from the showroom of the Lee Motor Company in beautiful downtown Monroeville.

His reddish brown hair, parted on the side, thick moustache and graying sideburns frame an infectious smile and reveal a childlike persona that may not seem to fit someone in his 50s, but there is little that is typical about Fred. His is the kind of passion for life that comes from being seconds from death, and living to tell about it. Which Fred has done.

I met Fred when I was assigned to produce a health segment on him for the Christian Broadcasting Network. After suffering a massive heart attack a few years earlier, Fred radically changed his diet and lifestyle, lost 143 pounds, and launched an annual bike race to raise money for cancer research.

When I met him, I had no idea that Fred would one day be the conduit for me to meet one of the truly iconic American authors of all time, one that few people outside Monroeville have had the chance to meet. When he first suggested it, I chuckled, thinking it would be impossible. I had heard tales of authors and Pulitzer-prize winning journalists attempting the same thing, and falling short–but Fred Kelley doesn't know the meaning of the word impossible.

Two years earlier, Fred carried 310 pounds on his 5'10" frame. One afternoon, he went to lunch with a co-worker, where he had a Quarter Pounder and large fries, washing them down with a supersized Coke. On the way back to work, Fred began having chest pains. His friend became so concerned that he took him to the Monroe County General Hospital. There, he was taken to the emergency room, where the doctors confirmed that Fred was having a massive heart attack.

They prepared to transfer him to a hospital in Mobile, about 90 miles away, and the doctors told his family not to hold out too much hope. But Fred caught a glimpse of his 12-year old daughter crying in the parking lot at Monroe County General Hospital as the ambulance pulled away. The sight gave him the will to live. Fred had already lost his wife to cancer two years earlier and wasn't about to let his daughter grow up without a birth parent. It wasn't easy but he survived, and over the next year and a half, made radical changes to his diet and lifestyle, losing 138 pounds.

One afternoon during his transformation, Fred exhorted the listeners of the Phil and Fred Show to pledge $1,000 for a cancer fundraiser before he signed off the air. It was twenty minutes before the show ended. If they did, Fred promised, he would ride his bicycle from the square in Monroeville to the U.S.S. Alabama. The callers responded and raised $1,000, so Fred was forced to make good on his promise. He bought a bike and began training. Within two years, Fred also turned the ride into an event, "Peddlin' for a Cure," which raises money for cancer research each year on Good Friday.

Besides Fred, there are two other Monroeville natives who also put the town on the map. Monroeville's claim to fame comes from its literary legacy, an unusual thing for a tiny industrial town of fewer than 5,000 residents. Both of these Monroeville natives were acclaimed novelists: Miss Nelle Harper Lee and her childhood friend, Truman Capote.

Capote passed away in 1984, but the mercurial "Miss Nelle" as they call her, was then still living in Monroeville. She had never published a book after *To Kill a Mockingbird*, and that fact has caused consternation for literature lovers everywhere. She also had never addressed the question, partly due to the fact that she had not given an interview in over 40 years.

Friends and acquaintances in the town were very protective of Miss Nelle and her privacy over the years. As a result, requests from potential biographers, television producers, newspaper reporters, and the like had pretty much all been summarily dismissed by her sister and lawyer Alice. Despite this, author Charles Shields was able to assemble a fascinating portrait of Nelle, drawn primarily from secondary sources and the few acquaintances in the town who were willing to open up to him, in his book, *Mockingbird: A Portrait of Harper Lee*. When news of his book reached Nelle and Alice who, at 100, was still practicing law, a decree went forth from the two of them that the author was not to be spoken to, and most of their friends and family obliged.

Stories have circulated about Nelle walking out of social gatherings when someone dared breach the taboo subject of her writing. Other times, she has been downright curmudgeonly and even cursed at literary interlopers. So it was obvious why I reacted with more than a little trepidation when Mr. Fred Kelley told me he could arrange for me to meet her.

Harper Lee was not always this reclusive of course. She traveled with Truman to Kansas to help him do research for *In Cold Blood*. Although she has always lived in Monroeville, she often visited New York to see Truman, and she was happy to attend cocktail parties, do interviews, and was an integral part of the literary scene. Something happened however, with the phenomenal success of *To Kill a Mockingbird* and she began to withdraw. She undoubtedly felt the intense pressure to match the critical and commercial success of the book and perhaps she didn't have it in her to try to duplicate it. Perhaps the press treated her unfairly in some manner and this was her response. Whatever the reason, she stopped giving interviews in the late 1960s. Those close to her say Truman's death in 1984 greatly affected her. Did she see how Truman had suffered so for his art, drinking himself to death when he could not produce, and decide that, for her, it was simply not worth it?

Nelle's reclusive nature was paradoxical considering how many things in the town surround her and Truman. Monroeville of course, *is* Maycomb, the setting for *Mockingbird*, and the town still retains much of the quaint character of the town that appears in the pages of *Mockingbird*: the rows of pecan trees, the quaint antebellum homes with screened-in porches where southern belles still sit on large rockers and sip iced tea, and where the businessmen in town still wear seersucker suits and wide brimmed hats. And of course, there is the courthouse. When the movie, *To Kill a Mockingbird*, starring Gregory Peck, was green-lighted, the studio sent Hollywood set designers to Monroeville so they could study and build an exact replica of the Monroe County Courthouse when they returned to Hollywood.

Each spring, a live play version is performed in and around the courthouse, and attendees are even invited to be jury members for the courthouse scenes. If Monroeville is a type of Mecca of southern literature, then the Monroe County Courthouse is the literary Dome of the Rock.

After I produced my segment on Fred, he and I stayed in touch. In the summer of 2011, he invited me to be on his show to talk about a new book I had written on country music. I was invited to talk about the book for an hour on Fred's show, but between the visits from animal rescue workers, clergymen heralding fish fries, locals touting yard sales, and merchants talking up their sales for the weekend, and a few tunes from the Platters and the Ink Spots, I got fifteen minutes at best. My fifteen minutes of fame in Monroeville. A few of the locals did, however, come by and purchase books from me.

When I packed up my books and started to bid farewell to Fred, however, he informed me that he had one more assignment for me. "Not so fast. I know you used to teach English, so I can't let you get out of Monroeville without meeting Harper Lee," he said.

My reaction was a combination of excitement mixed with stark terror. "I can't, Fred. I have to get back on the road. Besides, I wouldn't want to upset her," I said.

"Just sit down and I'll make a few calls for you. I know everybody in this town and they'll do anything for me," Fred said. "I know a girl that works where she is staying."

After dialing a few numbers, Fred finally reached a manager at the assisted living facility where Miss Nelle is living and spoke to her for a minute or so, then turned to me.

"OK, here's what you need to do. You take this lady a copy of your book. She is a big country music fan, so she will really appreciate it. She's going to act like your mother is looking for a facility and she's going to take you on a tour," he chortled. "And while you are on there, she's going to swing by Nelle's room and, if she's there, she's going to introduce you to her."

When I began to consider the number of people who have attempted this same act and been brushed aside like so many flies, I nearly started shaking.

"But what if she doesn't want to meet me?" I said. "What if she is in one of her moods?"

"Don't worry about it," Fred reassured me. "Just tell her you used to teach English and you're a big fan. You may even want to give her a copy of your book, too. Just don't ask her why she never wrote another one!" Fred laughed and slapped his knee.

I agreed to the terms of the meeting, but was still almost visibly shaking as he handed me the directions to the facility. Then Fred began giggling, "And while you are there, if the ladies are having their lunch, I want you to grab a Club cracker out of the basket and start munching on it—then you can tell all your friends back in Tennessee that you had lunch with Harper Lee!" he cackled.

I chuckled and headed out the door. I was not, under any circumstances, going to offer the author of a Pulitzer-prize winning novel a copy of my *Chicken Soup for the Soul: Country Music* edition.

Within minutes, I was sitting in the parking lot of the facility, a brand new, multi-unit home with bright yellow siding that offered services for residents that ranged from totally independent to assisted living, and a nursing facility in the back for those who were incapable of caring for themselves.

As I sat in the parking lot, I wondered how the idea of meeting an 85-year old woman could so incapacitate me. It was as if I were meeting Elvis, or the President, or Michael Jackson, or some foreign dignitary.

I finally mustered up the courage to walk inside, where I was met by Mary, the woman who would be giving me my 'tour." I tried to appear innocent, but I still felt like a stalker.

It was about noon when Mary showed me around, and most of the ladies were, as Fred had predicted, in the center of the facility, eating lunch. Mary played along and told me all about the services and rates, and asked me about my mother's condition and her meds, to which I mumbled something about bursitis or arthritis, or phlebitis, or some other kind of 'itus' as my eyes scanned the room for a white-haired women who resembled the one I had seen in pictures over the years.

When we had been on the tour for perhaps ten minutes, Mary leaned over to me and whispered, "See the lady in the pink sweater sitting by herself? That's her." I tried to be as unobtrusive as possible, but eventually turned my gaze in that general direction. At the moment, our eyes met, Miss Nelle had a mouth full of pasta of some sort, and the Alfredo sauce was dribbling down her chin. Then she scowled at me. I didn't know what to do. Would she know that I knew who she was, and scamper back to her room? Should I try to engage her in conversation, or just say 'hello'? Instead, I just stood there like a mouse that has come upon a snake and is paralyzed with fear.

I knew I couldn't come this far without at least trying to engage her, though. As I glided across the room peering at the walls and ceiling of the facility, pretending to analyze the ability of the structure to withstand tornadoes, I chatted with Mary some more. As I got closer and closer to Miss Nelle, the thoughts kept running through my mind, like *Do you realize how few people have been able to get this close to her?* I also thought, *This is the woman who wrote the book that's required reading of every high school kid in America, a book that had a hand in ending segregation in the South and changing the culture of a nation!*

A moment later, we were right beside her. I tried to think of some way to engage her in conversation, to say something totally unrelated to literature or writing, about the weather or the news, or politics—something that might allow her to drop her defenses and open up. Perhaps she would even invite me to sit down and chat with her. I had heard that if you caught her on a good day, when her faculties were clear and her mind alert, she could be quite pleasant, as long as you didn't bring up you-know-what.

I looked down at Miss Nelle Harper Lee. The scowl began to abate; the furrowed brows un-furrowed, and I saw something that almost resembled a smile beginning to creep from the corners of her mouth. I was still tongue-tied and my tour guide finally broke the silence.

"Good afternoon, Miss Nelle," Mary said. I smiled at her, trying to reassure her that I was not a member of the paparazzi in disguise, or a rogue reporter trying to trap her. She heard Mary's question, but never took her eyes off me. Finally, I gathered my courage to speak. "Hi. How are you today?" I chimed in. Nelle continued staring at me and finally, the corners of her mouth turned up and she smiled. Then she nodded at me.

That's all I got. A nod and a grin.

A moment later, Mary led me away. I watched as the author of one of the greatest works of literature in the English language wiped Alfredo sauce off her chin.

I thanked Mary and headed out the door, still feeling like a stalker. I couldn't resist casting one last glimpse, however, back at Miss Nelle, who was staring out the window.

The whole way back to Nashville, I rehashed the encounter in my mind, trying to think of some way that I could have interjected something into our brief interaction that might have made a connection, that might have made her invite me to sit down and chat. To accomplish what nearly all of the hundreds of journalists over the past 50 years have been unable to do.

In one scene in my mind, I fantasized about breaking away from Mary and grabbling Miss Nelle by the shoulders and shouting, "For God's sake woman, please, tell me why you never wrote another book!" (Of course, I discovered a couple of years after meeting Nelle that she had, indeed, written at least one other work, *Go Set a Watchmen*, published in 2015, which was possibly written before *Mockingbird*, but I was unaware of that at the time.)

In another scenario, I imagined myself plopping down and chatting with her about nursing homes or the weather or politics, in the hopes that I might eventually get her to open up and share a little about her life.

But alas, I had done neither.

Now it is spring of 2016 and, as I am doing the final proofs on this collection of essays, I see several news stories online announcing that Miss Nelle has gone on to her reward, at the age of 89. So the hope of ever returning to Monroeville for another meeting with Ms. Nelle Harper Lee has been dashed, although our brief meeting may be the kind of story I will be able to tell to my grandchildren.

Now I suppose I will have to find another literary recluse to begin stalking. Perhaps one afternoon, I will rent a convertible and make my way down the Natchez Trace Parkway to Oxford Mississippi, swing by the home of William Faulkner, then pick out a few titles at Square Books, then try to track down that other Oxford writer, John Grisham, who has not given an interview in decades.

Maybe I will even take Fred Kelley along for the ride.

DESPERATELY SEEKING NORMAN

*"The ideal of your soul, the thing that it yearns
for, is not more knowledge. It is not interested in
comparison, or winning, or light, or ownership—
or not even happiness. The ideal of your soul
is space, expansion, immensity–and the one
thing it needs more than anything else is to be
free to expand, to reach out, and to embrace the
infinite. Why? Because the soul is infinity itself."*

WAYNE DYER

In the summer of 1996, I hopped an Amtrak train bound
for Seattle. The trip would last a total of two weeks: three
days each way on the train itself, coupled with a week in
between to explore the western half of Washington, the Ho
Rain Forrest, and Mt. Rainier.

I had two reasons for wanting to take this excur-
sion. At the time, I desperately needed to cash in a
"get-out-of-relationship-free" card and I thought this would
be the best way to do so. The Internet was still in its infancy

and not everyone had cell phones, so it was the perfect way to disconnect from both the culture at large and my girlfriend.

I was only in my mid-thirties, but I had already grown tired of so many things. The bloom was already off the rose of my still fledgling teaching career. Like many idealistic young English majors, I had visions of being Mr. Keating from *Dead Poets Society*, changing the lives of students by exhorting them to 'carpe diem'—seize the day—and follow their bliss. But instead of John Keating, I ended up more like the character George Caldwell from John Updike's novel *The Centaur*, trying to salvage an out-of-control class long enough to spit out my lesson each day. Unfortunately, the rigors of teaching four or five sections of composition a semester for seven years to eighteen-year olds, many of whom admittedly didn't even want to be in college, but weren't sure what else to do with their lives at that point, had destroyed what little creativity and inventiveness I had in the classroom in my first few years, and resulted in my becoming disillusioned and despondent.

I had grown tired of correcting the same errors on hundreds of papers, tired of sitting in the same faculty meetings every week, tired of going to the same conferences where no one seems to really learn anything of value, and tired of preparing the same course materials from the same syllabi every semester. I had also grown tired of dead-end relationships, and I just needed some time alone. And there's no better way to reflect and get clear than by hopping on a train for three weeks.

My second reason for the trip was due to the influence of a little memoir I had just read called *A River Runs Through It*. I had also recently seen the Robert Redford-produced film of the same name, and was smitten by not only the quality of Norman Maclean's writing, but also the majesty of the land where this movie was shot. I wanted to discover this land of the great trout rivers that Maclean wrote about, and see it up close. The area had been beckoning me for several months, and I knew it was time I heeded its siren song.

There is a scene from the film that I could not get out of my mind. In it, Norman and his brother Paul are small boys and are running through a spectacular Montana meadow, carefree and laughing, as the majestic snow-capped peaks of the Gallatin Mountain Range in the distance. As the young boys frolic in their innocence surrounded by the glory of creation, we hear Redford's voiceover describing Norman Maclean's childhood. "Every afternoon, I was set free, untutored and untouched until supper to learn on my own the natural side of God's order. And there could be no better place to learn that than the Montana of my youth. It was a world with dew still on it, more touched by wonder and possibility than any I have since known."

So with the dream of being a successful songwriter in Nashville having already faded into the sunset years before, and feeling unfulfilled in my second career as an English professor, coupled with the fact that I couldn't seem to find any female relationships of any depth, I set out for the Northwest. Perhaps while nestled in the mountainous,

pine-covered country of Maclean's youth, I, too, would redis-
cover that sense of infinite possibility that one only feels in
the unencumbered innocence of youth.

In some sense, Normal Maclean had become a kind of
a surrogate father for me, although I had never met him.
Through the pages of his books, I got to know Maclean as
well as I knew my dad. Ironically, my father and Norman
Maclean actually looked alike. Although my father was an
avid reader well into his eighties, his formal education had
ceased after ninth grade. They were similar in other ways,
though: both were lean, hardened men, but both had a
sensitive side that could be revealed if you knew the right
combination to their psychic tumblers. In an NPR interview with Maclean shortly before his death, the interviewer
takes a walk with him to his cabin in Montana, where the
two sit down and share a glass of bourbon. In his voiceover,
the interviewer describes Maclean this way: "He still seems
physically almost menacing. This is a retired English professor we're talking about."

With this mindset, I set off on my pilgrimage to find
myself, or perhaps an archetypal father, figure out what I
wanted to do with my life career-wise or, at the very least,
discover the land that inspired one of my favorite books and
in the process perhaps reclaim some of the lost passion of
my youth.

I boarded the City of New Orleans train in the small
town of Newbern, Tennessee, just northeast of Memphis, at
the crisp hour of 12:30 a.m., the only time the train runs

through the town. From there, I would go to Chicago, stop for a six-hour layover, then catch the Empire Builder train, which runs along the Canadian border in northern Montana and the northern tip of Idaho, before it turns south into the Seattle area.

The return route would be a different one, the Pioneer, which winds southeast out of Seattle, through Oregon and into Colorado and the plains states then on to Chicago. There, I would once again transfer to the City of New Orleans train back to Newbern, get my car, and drive back to Nashville.

The lyrics to Steve Goodman's song that was inspired by the route ran through my mind as I boarded the train and settled in. "All along the southbound Odyssey, the train pulls out at Kankakee / and rolls along past houses farms, and fields. / Passing trains that have no names / and freight yards full of old black men / and the graveyards of the rusted automobiles."

I found myself humming the chorus as I gazed at the scenery. With Goodman's melody in my head and the images created by Maclean's book in my mind, I watched the land-scapes pass by as the train rolled on through Tennessee and Illinois.

A private sleeping room was quite costly, so I opted for the regular passenger fare. At night, the chair would recline and the porter would bring pillows and blankets for us. I would take several sponge baths in the train bath-room in lieu of a shower. It wasn't the ideal way to travel, but it was still very scenic and, at the time, I figured the extra $400 could be better spent getting a rental car and touring the states of Washington and Montana for a few days once I arrived.

The fellow travelers I met on the train included an older, bearded gentleman who literally lived on the train for several months a year. He did accounting work, and would have FedEx packages waiting for him at various stops along the way. He hated sitting in an office, he said, and this way he could write off his trips. As I recall, he had a particular fascination with waterfalls. Each time he would see that we were about to pass one, he would run to the lower level of the car and lean out the window to photograph it.

Others included a young college girl who said she was on her way to Mexico, where she did missionary work every year. Another lady had just left her husband for a lesbian lover she had met through a dating website.

I did purchase the dining plan, so every evening, I would put on long pants, spray on some cologne, and head for the dining car, where I would have a nice glass of merlot and wait for my meal. The dining car had a glass ceiling, which allowed for a more panoramic view of the Rockies and was breathtaking. Often times, I would bring my copy of *River* and some works of criticism on Maclean to the dining car to read while I waited for dinner.

I've always wondered why some books resonate with so many readers as strongly as *A River Runs Through It* was one that affected me on many levels. It is a short but powerful account of Maclean's early life in Montana and the death of his brother Paul. Maclean's father was a Presbyterian minister and the biblical allusions and recurring motif of fly-fishing are repeated throughout the book. Despite its length (just a little over 100 pages), it is regarded as one of the great works of memoir of the 20th century. I read my copy at least two more times during that trip. After we left Chicago and traveled along the Canadian border and through North Dakota, eventually to the gradual ascent up the eastern slopes of the Rockies as we approached Montana, I was mesmerized by the views from the train of the rippling waters and trout streams that Maclean describes in his book, literally only feet away from me.

When the University of Chicago Press first published it in 1976, the title *A River Runs Through It: And Other Stories* was a bit problematic. At the time, the genre of memoir was not as well-defined as it is today, and the subtitle led some distributors and chains to categorize it as fiction, even though the three stories were works of memoir from Maclean's youth. His prose is clean and sparse, almost Hemingway-like—no doubt a result of his father's constant emphasis on the importance of revision and on the economy of language.

In the foreword to the 25th anniversary edition of the book, published in 2001, Annie Proulx shares her own story of encountering the book for the first time shortly after its initial publication. She bought the book at O'Hare airport and began reading it on the plane but later picked it up and finished it on the front porch of her farmhouse in Burlington, Vermont. "There are few books that have the power to put the reader in such a deep trance that the real world literally falls away," Proulx writes. "When I read the last line, 'I am haunted by waters,' I sighed and looked up. It was deepening twilight. In the long grass at the end of the porch, perhaps twenty feet distant, stood an uncommonly large bobcat, staring at me. It made no movement except for a slight twitching of its upward-curved tail. Such was the power of the story, that I was still in the arctic half-light of the canyon, and the bobcat seemed on the bank of the river that runs through all things, and there it stayed, forever joined in my mind to Maclean's story." She later writes, "It is one of the rare, truly great stories in American literature—allegory, requiem, and memoir."

Despite its simplicity, *River* seems to grab the reader by the throat and won't let loose until he or she finishes it. Perhaps it's the way the book rekindles memories of childhood for those was fortunate enough to have been raised in a rural environment. Perhaps it's the vivid imagery of the Pacific Northwest and the semi-fantasy world of fly-fishing. Maybe it was the personality of Maclean himself, and the stern grand-fatherly image that he evoked. Or perhaps it's the universal theme of loss that has helped make the book a commercial and critical success for over 35 years. Then again, maybe it's just the power of his writing.

It is puzzling that, during his tenure as a professor of literature at the University of Chicago, Maclean wrote relatively few academic essays before writing *River*, which was really his first book-length work, and then did so only after he retired. In the interviews I've listened to, and a few that I've seen on video, Maclean seems both approachable and intimidating at the same time. I could easily picture myself sitting in his cabin, sipping bourbon with him, discussing literature into the wee hours of the morning.

I grew up on a river, so anytime a book has a river as its setting, I am drawn to it. Rivers can be so awe-inspiring and yet, command great respect. As I understand, Maclean was like that as well. I only have a few memories of my own father from childhood, but they include the times we spent fishing for catfish on the banks of the Ohio River together.

Rivers also have the ability to transport one back in time. Perhaps the archetypal motif of the river transports us all back to the Fertile Crescent: the Tigris and Euphrates at the dawn of civilization. In literature, the river sometimes symbolizes death or rebirth.

During my train trip, *A River Runs Through It* served as my tour guide. Over those two weeks. I spent time pondering everything from my current career trajectory to my inability to sustain relationships, to the bigger existential questions surrounding life and meaning and purpose. When I got to Seattle and got a rental car, I started driving with no particular destination in mind, but I spent several of those days in the Ho Rain Forrest and on Mt. Rainier. I spent hours each day journaling. I would read, take naps, go for a walk—whatever I felt like. In the evening, I would often sit by one of the many rivers flowing through the Olympic Mountain range, writing, thinking, sometimes just staring at the awesome beauty.

The thing I remember most about that time was the sustained peace, uninterrupted by phone calls and emails and voice mail messages. In one of the early chapters in *River*, Maclean's father tells Norman to listen to the sound of the waters—this is where you can hear the voice of God.

I would love to say that I came back from that trip with profound new revelations about life and career and faith and relationships, but I can't. I stayed out of relationships for some time after that. For whatever reason, they always seemed too draining for me. I did realize that what I thought was a fear of commitment was probably just a fear of committing to the wrong person. I taught for a few more years, but that summer, I realized I would not do it for the rest of my career. For all the intellectual stimulating and rare moments when I actually touched a student in some way with my insights, I realized this vocation was not my "calling."

Over decades later, I still recall the peace I felt after finally learning to quiet my mind.. Perhaps it was this peace that enabled Maclean to write such powerful prose. It's not a coincidence that all of the world's religions place such an emphasis on quieting the mind and meditating. It is a state that I began to crave upon my return, and I've learned to make it a priority, even if it means putting up a sign that says "In a meeting," on my office door and sneaking off for a walk at nearby Percy Warner Park. For the rest of my time at the college, when bombarded by texts and emails and voice-mails, I would close my office door and put the sign up long enough to meditate and get centered for a while. Often, I would return to those memories of Montana, where I would find refreshment for my soul.

Quantum physicists say the energy field from which matter comes into existence, is a cosmic soup that some call the "unified field." It is here that energy decides what type of matter it wants to become, and, through the organizing intelligence that many believe is God, waves become particles and then atoms and molecules. This field is comprised of pure intelligence waiting to be born. It is the "missing link" between energy and matter: an invisible, organizing intelligence that can mold atoms into molecules of steel, or oxygen, or a piece of human skin. At that level, everything is pure potential. And anything is possible.

I still harken back to that peaceful world of Maclean's youth, and the glistening trout streams and the snow-capped peaks, as well as to my own boyhood world on the Ohio River. And I can still hear Robert Redford's voice narrating, "It was a world with dew still on it, *more touched by wonder and possibility than any I have since known.*

Isn't that the world we are all seeking?

I have read the closing words of *A River Runs Through It* perhaps a hundred times: "Then in the Arctic half-light of the canyon," Maclean writes, "all existence fades to a being with my soul and memories and the sounds of the Big Blackfoot River and a four-count rhythm and the hope that a fish will rise. Eventually, all things merge into one, and a river runs through it. The river was cut by the world's great flood and runs over rocks from the basement of time. On some of those rocks are timeless raindrops. Under the rocks are the words, and some of the words are theirs . . ."

On my trek to the Northwest that summer, I learned to be quiet enough to not only listen to, but to *hear*, those words.

CAPOTE AND ME

*"On the night of November 14, two men broke into
a quiet farmhouse in Kansas and murdered an
entire family. Why did they do that? Two worlds
exist in this country: the quiet, conservative
life and the life of those two men . . . and
those worlds converged that bloody night."*

TRUMAN CAPOTE, **IN COLD BLOOD**

*"Researching this work has changed my
life. It's altered my point of view about
almost everything. And I think those who
read it will be similarly affected."*

CAPOTE

In the summer of 1989, I was enrolled in a graduate class
on the American novel at Tennessee State University
in Nashville. The class was taught by Dr. Clayton Reeve, an

amiable fellow then in his mid-50s with short, stringy, blond hair and a thin nose, who frequently paced around the room with his forefinger and thumb on his chin—in the "thinker" position—as he lectured. Dr. Reeve served on my thesis committee and we later became friends.

After being re-introduced to Faulkner's Benjy, Fennimore Cooper's Natty Bumpo and various other notable characters in American literature, most of whom I had encountered in my undergraduate days but actually enjoyed reading this time, we moved on to a little paperback with the intriguing title *In Cold Blood*. I had read *Breakfast at Tiffany's* and was familiar with some of Capote's short stories, but had never read this particular work.

That year I did. But I didn't just read it; I devoured it, and have done so many times since. This little $13.95 paperback significantly altered the trajectory of my teaching career and writing ambitions. I was, in Capote's words, "similarly affected," by reading this work as he was in writing it.

I was three or four chapters into the book when I asked Dr. Reeve, "Is this fiction or nonfiction?"

"Yes," he answered chuckling.

It read like fiction; yet it was based on actual events. The course was a fiction course, and everything we had read up to this point had been fiction, which made this novel even more peculiar. But what would you call it? Was this a true crime novel? No. Was it journalism? It read too descriptively for that. And if it was true, how did Capote do it? How did he know what Dick Hickock had for breakfast the day he murdered the Clutters, or what Perry Smith's sister and mother were like? How did he know Dick's pet nicknames for Perry, or what they were wearing when they went to Mexico? Surely he had embellished a little—or had he?

I peppered Reeve with questions like these. The type of research I had done up to that point—literary research—usually consisted of poring over dusty old texts and letters in a dimly lit corner of a library. I had no idea that someone could research by interviewing murderers on Death Row for years at a time. Talk about primary sources.

I had no idea that this type of research was even possible, that a writer could recreate dialogue that occurred twenty years before, or unveil the innermost thoughts and details about a subject's personality, and pass it off as nonfiction. It's exactly what Capote had done. But was that, you know, *allowed?*

Capote may not have actually invented this "new form, the nonfiction novel," as he claimed, but he certainly catapulted the genre. In the book, Capote presents us with this portrait of two murderers with such power and compelling clarity that it is almost physically jarring at times. It is not unlike seeing a train wreck—simultaneously intriguing and terrifying. Part of me wanted to put the book down in revulsion and another part of me wanted to continue to stare on in obsessive disbelief.

> *"He (Clutter) was just looking at me, looking into my eyes, like he expected me to kill him.*

Like he expected me to be the kind of person who would kill him. All I was thinking was, 'This nice man is scared of me.' I was so ashamed. I thought he was a very nice, gentle, man. And I thought so right up 'til I slit his throat."

PERRY SMITH

I discovered, of course, after researching both the book and Capote further that everything in it was completely accurate, based on his years of interviewing Hickock and Smith while they were in prison. The text is so much more than a gratuitous account of the grisly murder of the Clutter family —in fact, very little of the book centers on the actual night of the murder. Instead, it is an attempt by Capote to make *sense* of the murders and the murderers. Capote felt drawn to Perry Smith, one of the accused, partly due to the fact that the two men had somewhat similar backgrounds.

But Capote also wrote *In Cold Blood* because he wanted to understand Truman. The whole experience was so terrifying and draining, however, that it left him physically, mentally, and emotionally exhausted. So much so that he never wrote another complete work.

Lee Gutkind, sometimes called the "Godfather of Creative Nonfiction," who also founded the journal of the same name at Pittsburgh, uses the metaphor of the tour guide for the creative nonfiction writer. In this genre, the writer leads the reader on a journey of self-discovery. Along the way, the effective guide comments on areas of interest, but also allows the guided, the reader, to enjoy the experience for himself. Unlike the academic essay and other forms of didactic writing, this type of writing does not always seek to convince or persuade, but rather to share, and perhaps to enlighten. I liked that.

In his introduction to the collection of environmental narratives, *On Nature*, Gutkind relates a story of an Outward-Bound experience in which he leads a group of hikers out of the wilderness. He writes, "In some aspects, creative nonfiction writers undergo ordeals as demanding, difficult, and subsequently rewarding as Outward Bound every day."

He adds, "Books and essays are mountains of mystery, causing inconceivable struggle and great bursts of physical and intellectual energy. Because the genre is so demanding, requiring story (a narrative framework), scene (dialogue, description, characterization, etc. . .), action (drama, suspense), *and* information (factual content), a creative nonfiction writer is constantly bushwhacking through unfamiliar and frustratingly elusive terrain. Most of the time, the struggle is worth it and both writer and reader are rewarded."

Other critics and authors have used the tour guide metaphor when describing creative nonfiction. Kristen Iversen, author of *The Unsinkable Molly Brown* and *Shadow Boxing* (and one of my writing professors at the University of Memphis), writes, "A good essayist takes the reader on a journey, defining and commenting upon a real-life experience or observation in a detailed and insightful manner that leads to a broader understanding of life and a greater sense of meaning or self-fulfillment. The responsibility of the writer lies in showing a connection or intersection of personal experience with the larger world."

Throughout *In Cold Blood*, Capote serves as this tour guide, standing on the side of the tour group, commenting and leading us through this journey into the dark psychic jungle of two men, in cinematic chapters, showing us the eerie caverns and crevasses we may not want to see, but need to know exist. Capote's portrayal of the idyllic, peaceful, Kansas wheat country of the Clutter family, and the violent world of Hickock and Smith—and the collision of those two worlds—is simply masterful, and also why the book is still considered a classic 50 years after its publication.

In one scene from *Capote*, the feature film based on the writing of *In Cold Blood*, Capote (Philip Seymour Hoffman) is sitting with his editor, when the editor turns to him and says, "This book is going to change everything. It's going to change how people read your writing. I think it's going to change how people *write*."

> "...afterward, the townspeople, theretofore
> sufficiently unfearful of each other to seldom
> trouble to lock their doors, found fantasy recreating
> (the murders) over and over again—those somber
> explosions that stimulated fires of mistrust in
> the glare of which many old neighbors now
> viewed each other strangely, and as strangers."

CAPOTE, *IN COLD BLOOD*

As the convicted murderers' appeal process began to drag on, Capote found himself in a moral dilemma: he had to know the ending to finish the book, but the ending would not come until two men were either released on a legal technicality or ended up dangling at the end of a rope. Sentencing had already been handed down, so life imprisonment was not an option at this point. It would be either acquittal or death. Neither of the possibilities comforted Capote.

> *"It's as if Perry and I grew up in the same house. Then one day, he stood up and went out the back door and I went out the front."*

CAPOTE

It was in Clayton Reeve's classroom in that I decided I wanted to write essays and reportage. It wasn't until five years that I even began to research MFA programs that offered creative nonfiction concentrations, another five years before I even applied to one, and still another five to work my way through the program part-time and finish my thesis.

But then a funny thing happened. I starting getting some of my essays and creative nonfiction published. I had written hundreds of magazine articles up to this point, but almost no literary essays. Even the rejection slips began coming back with words of encouragement.

A number of my friends and acquaintances were accomplished fiction writers. Since I had always considered that the highest form of the art, I tried to write fiction for years even though it felt unnatural and forced. The results were predictably trite and formulaic. I loved reading fiction, so I couldn't figure out why I wasn't able to write fiction. Once, I holed myself up in a mountain chalet for several days trying to finish a short story I had begun years before. I struggled the entire long weekend and came back with a worse story than the one I took there with me.

But now, in creative nonfiction, essay, and memoir, I found a genre that I loved writing as well as reading. It never felt forced, and I never ran out of ideas. Even when I wrote magazine pieces, I found myself incorporating many of the techniques I was learning about in creative nonfiction. I was so excited to know that I could be free of the "who, what, when, where, and why" prison of journalism and the stifling shackles of the inverted pyramid.

I had found my genre.

I started reading the *Best American Essays* series and reportage works like *Midnight in the Garden of Good and Evil, Friday Night Lights,* and *Seabiscuit;* works of memoir like *A River Runs Through It, Angela's Ashes,* and *All Over But the Shoutin';* essay collections by David Sedaris, Lee Gutkind, Gay Talese, and the literary journalism of John McPhee.

But there was another side trip on this journey of self-discovery that began with *In Cold Blood* that endeared me to Capote. Like him, I had grown up in a small, industrial town, raised by two working-class parents who seldom spoke to each other without quarreling, although it was never a particularly violent environment. My father worked as a clay miner, a brickyard worker, and a house painter, and my mother was a waitress and later, stay-at-home mother.

On my father's side, however, there was constant drama. One of my cousins was accused and convicted of shooting the woman who was his estranged wife at the time. There are conflicting accounts as to whether it was an accident, a crime of passion, or murder, but he served nearly 20 years. When he was finally released from prison for good behavior he was accused, again, some say falsely, of another crime. Vowing never to go back to prison, he hung himself in his jail cell with his belt.

Years earlier, his brother, after numerous run-ins with the law, was killed when he tried to beat a train at a railroad crossing. When I grew up, and even today, there were stories about relatives on that side of the family that involve everything from petty theft to moonshine and drug running, assault, and various other crimes.

As a young man, I often wondered the same thing that Capote did. How was it that these relatives of mine, raised in the same town, with similar parents and similar peers, who went to the same schools and lived in the same neighborhoods, took such a different path in life? Why did they get up and walk out the back door, while my brother and sister and I walked out the front? Studying Capote's works and his life helped me confront the same tough questions he had posed.

"More tears are shed over answered
prayers than unanswered ones."

<small>Capote's foreword to his</small>
<small>last, unfinished novel.</small>

Like many fans of his, I wonder what Capote could have done had he lived another twenty years. He was a relatively young man, still in his 50s, when he died of liver disease. Did he simply write himself out, with *In Cold Blood?* His childhood friend, Nelle Harper Lee, wrote *To Kill a Mockingbird,* but never wrote another book. It still confounds many literary critics. Was there a connection? Did Harper Lee decide that this "inconceivable struggle" was simply too much for her? Could it be that she, after seeing the torment that *In Cold Blood* and its aftermath wreaked on her boyhood friend, decided that the writing, for all of its benefits, was simply not worth the cost?

When I was younger, getting published and receiving some sort of acclaim was all I concerned myself with, but after reading Capote, I began reading more and writing for the love of it, for the self-discovery, which is the only real reason anyone should read or write. The writing itself became reward enough.

If the recent popularity of reality TV shows is teaching us anything about America, it's that we all have a little but of voyeur in us. We are desperate for connection. After decades of rugged individualism and independence, it now seems we are intrigued with the prospect of peering into one another's lives—even the lives that are not glamorous or particularly significant. It's the contact, the shared humanity that we crave. Anne Dillard called it "waking up" to the world around us, to the mystery and awe of others, as well as to the natural world around us, after a half century of cultural obsession with self.

We are awakening to the fascinating lives of others around us and hearing the compelling stories they have to share. And this new literature is a big part of what is reconnecting us, coaxing us along on this path of discovery, the kind that Capote began leading me on over twenty years ago.

And that is what I love about creative nonfiction.

WATCHING DONALD DIE

This quiet dust, was gentleman and ladies
And lads and girls—
Was laughter and ability and sighing
And frocks and curls;
This passive place a summer's nimble mansion
Where bloom and bees
Fulfilled their oriental circuit
Then ceased like these.

EMILY DICKINSON

I was fifty years old the first time I watched someone die. On November 7, 2008, my wife Clare, along with her mother, her sister and brother-in-law, and I sat keeping a vigil at the bedside of Donald Graydon Dunn at The Medical Center of Southeast Texas in Port Arthur. Three days earlier, Don has suffered a heart attack and passed out in his driveway. By the time the paramedics got there and revived him, his brain had been without oxygen for 15 minutes. He was

92 and the doctors told us there was very little brain activity. After much angst, the family made the decision to take him off life support.

Early in the morning, the nurse came in and explained the details to us in a very clinical manner. I know health care professionals deal with such things on a daily basis, but still, the casualness and sterile, professorial manner in which she delivered her lecture seemed so academic, it seemed as though she were addressing a class of nursing students rather than a family.

Driving through downtown Groves, Texas that week, I felt an intense compassion for the hard-working people who settled this area and the simplicity of their lifestyles. The town is straight out of a Norman Rockwell painting. The local Rotary, Kiwanis and Lions Clubs sponsorship banners that hung over the outfield fence at the Little League baseball field in Groves revealed where the men who worked in the local DuPont plant spent most of their spare time. They were the first generation to enjoy a modicum of security—national, family, and job security—and it became the focus of their existence, and their children's as well. After growing up through the turmoil of the early 20th century, that's all they really wanted from life: to be able to show up and do a good day's work for a good day's pay, and have something tucked away for retirement; to know the company gates would still be open when they showed up the next morning; to be able to watch their kids play baseball in the local sandlots, and to be able to have a beer at the club with their buddies on weekends.

That's all.

When a man is not a celebrity, politician, athlete or other public figure, his death may not come with much fanfare, but it doesn't mean he did not touch many lives. For the nurses and hospital staff, it might be just another work day, but for the family, it's something remarkable: they are saying good-bye to the man who meant everything to them for half a century. Despite the fact that he grew up on a farm and spent most of his life in a factory, Donald lived a life full of culture and the arts, and richly savoring the time he spent with family and friends.

Mr. Dunn's four-score and twelve years spanned the most remarkable time period in the history of mankind. During his life, he saw the mass production of the automobile. He saw air travel advance from a thirty-second flight by two men in a crude single engine plane on the dunes of North Carolina to a super-sonic, transatlantic flight from New York to London in just over three hours. He saw the development of the interstate highway system, the telephone, personal comput-ers and the Internet. He witnessed the Great Depression and two World Wars, and watched a man walk on the moon. But his greatest thrill in his life, he always said, was watching his son and two girls grow up.

Donald was born in Marie, West Virginia in 1917, the year the U.S. entered World War I. Despite the incredible changes in the world around it, Marie is a place where time has stood still. It had then, and still has, perhaps 300 resi-dents. It is nestled in a quiet hollow just north of Princeton.

Most of the inhabitants were farmers then, although many of their progeny have moved on to other more lucrative cash crops, and substances created in crude home chemistry labs. It is unfortunate, but since the decline of farming in the area, the unemployment rate is now high, and distribution of drugs is often the only form of employment for many young men.

Don's father passed away when he was just five. His recollections of him are few, and Don soon became the little man of the household, taking care of his mother and two brothers. The loss of his father played a big part in Don's desire to have a vibrant, regular connection with his own children, which he fathered when he was in his late 40's, very unusual for that era.

When he turned 18, he applied for a job at the DuPont plant in Charleston, and was one of the fortunate few to be hired. As the country dug itself out of the Great Depression, Americans kept their eyes on a young private and his new political party in Germany who appeared to be re-industrializing and militarizing the fallen nation of Germany all over again.

After a few years at the Charleston plant, Don was offered a chance to transfer to the Orange, Texas DuPont plant and embraced this new journey with as much aplomb as he had his previous adventures, and began packing up his belongings and heading to the Gulf Coast.

Perhaps the most intriguing thing about Don was this eagerness to embrace new things. When one thinks of a young farm boy from the hills of West Virginia with only (at the time) a high school education, the picture that emerges is not usually someone who has a fondness for fine wines and single malt Scotches, local theater, classical music, and Broadway plays. But that was Don.

While at the Charleston plant, Don was never really understood by his co-workers. Many would probably have been hard-pressed to locate Manhattan on a map, let alone have any desire to travel there and watch a Broadway play. But Don, unmarried and unattached, had no hesitation in packing his suitcase, dusting off his one Brooks Brothers suit and wide-brimmed hat, and booking a seat on the Friday night train out of Charleston.

He often treated himself to dinner at the legendary Sardi's restaurant on Broadway, most certainly one of the venues where he acquired his taste for fine food and spirits, then taking advantage of the last minute ticket discounts on the Great White Way before turning in at one of the more affordable Inns in Midtown, catching an early Sunday train back to Charleston.

Don often shunned the typical passions and pastimes of his co-workers, whether they be guzzling beer, watching high school football, or listening to country or bluegrass music, not out of any sense of snobbery, or that he was above those things: they simply held no appeal for him. Other things, such as barn dances, or pot lucks at the local Methodist Church in Hinton, or simple drives through the country, were more acceptable.

These Broadway nights were certainly not weekly or even monthly experiences, mind you. But the fact that he sought out this unseen world, in pre-television days, without prompting and often without peers, says a lot about who he was and his desire to suck the marrow out of the bone of life even at an early age. The fact that he stayed single well into his thirties, another rejection of social convention in West Virginia, was one of the reasons he was able to enjoy these exotic mini-expeditions. I remember how thrilled he was when I called him one evening unexpectedly from Manhattan. I was attending a conference at the Grand Hyatt and called to let him know I'd just had a bowl of gumbo at the Grand Central Oyster Bar, another of his old Manhattan haunts, and a night cap at Sardi's. Since I heard so much about these places from him, I just had to investigate. He was almost giddy with a childlike glee for several minutes when I told him. I knew he was reliving his life in the post-war years.

Sometimes during these weekend jaunts, he would also wander over to Wall Street, and soon thereafter also developed a passion for finance and investing. The fact that he remained single later in life not only afforded him the opportunity to travel, but also to begin investing with his discretionary income. He began reading the *Wall Street Journal* and soon he was investing in stocks.

Don partnered with a friend from Charleston in pioneering what he hoped would become a chain of ladies specialty retail clothing stores. But World War II and a slowing economy kicked the legs out of that dream, and he and his partner were forced to sell the store after only a few years. When he was in his 90s, he and I would often sit up late after our wives had gone to bed, have a brandy together, and talk about stocks. On many of those evenings, his face would still light up as he went on in great detail about those years, his desire to learn the retail trade, registering with Dunn and Bradstreet, getting his business license, and the myriad other details that go into starting a business. He ended up staying with DuPont for virtually all of his working life, but I could tell when he spoke with so much passion about this season in his life, that he truly mourned the failure of that business.

During those late night conversations, I often shared with him my frustrations with teaching and my desire to write full-time. He often told me that would be a great thing to do—after I retired—that is. It often struck me as ironic that someone like Don, who had rolled the dice himself many times, taking risks with stocks, real estate, and even a retail business, would discourage someone else from pursuing his dreams. But then I realized this was the paradox of so many members of this Greatest Generation. They saw a grand vision for what their country could be, and what they could be as individuals, with the opportunities that abounded every-where around them, and yet were often so fixated on steady paychecks, medical insurance, retirement plans, pensions, social security, and 401Ks that they were frozen from acting on those individual visions, except possibly as an avocation, where they would not be risking anything. This seemed to be particularly true of the immigrants, farm workers, and others who had never really known financial security of any kind, and a job at 'the plant' with a steady paycheck, benefits, and a pension plan was something to be held onto with a death grip. It never lessoned my view of him, though. In his mind, I know he was simply looking out for the best interests of his daughters and grandchildren.

These and myriad other memories flooded over me, as the nurse entered the room and began giving instructions to the family as to how to proceed from here. After she gave the instructions, the nurse asked the family members if they wished to say anything more to him. His two daughters bent over and caressed the face of this man who had given them the gift of life, and said goodbye to him. Don's wife and his two son-in-laws did the same. Then the nurse leaned over, and in a sterile fashion, turned off the machine. For several moments, there was only the steady beep-beep-beep of the heart monitor. The staff had disconnected the jarring warning sound that the monitor makes in the event of a cardiac arrest, of course, to make the environment as peaceful as possible. The only other sound was an occasional sniffle from one of the girls.

"The monitor might show some brain activity for a while, but that's normal," the nurse said again in her clinical tone. For nearly a half an hour, the green line continued to register occasional peaks and valleys, and then the peaks got smaller and smaller and smaller. At one point the line went flat but no alarms sounded. There were now no sounds coming from his body, other than an occasional twitch or sudden movement that jarred the family members back to reality. We had all heard the stories of people, even elderly ones, who had been given no hope, but when removed from the respirator, somehow were jolted back to consciousness and survived for years. I know it passed through all of our minds at least once, but that slim hope faded with each minute that passed.

As far as ways to die, it was ideal, really—relatively pain-free and surrounded by loved ones—but there is still something haunting and unforgettable about final fare-wells, even when one has been preparing oneself to accept it.

When the green electronic blip finally went to flat and stayed there, my wife turned quickly to me, her eyes wide open as if to say, "It's *really* over now isn't it?" I reached out my arms and embraced her tightly for several minutes. Even until that morning, she could still caress her father's cheek and tell him she loved her one more time, with the slight hope that his hovering spirit might still be able to hear her.

But now it was over.

At that point, I too, broke down. I wanted more than any-thing to cover her heart and protect it from the pain, much as someone who has had a heart surgery holds a pillow to their heart when they cough to protect it from damage, but no amount of consolation could help. Her heart was break-ing, and there was nothing I could do other than hold her as her soft sobs eventually grew quieter on my shoulder. Even though I know closure can't be accomplished until grief is fully expressed, it's still difficult to watch a loved one go through it.

I've wondered many times since that morning, when it was that Mr. Dunn's life slipped from his body into the next life. When was the exact moment of death? Or perhaps there is no single moment; perhaps the soul lingers for minutes or hours, or even longer, while the body literally gives up the ghost. The doctors and nurses all seemed quite concerned with recording this exact moment, as well as his weight at the time of death, as if he would somehow be denied access to the next world if his records were not accurate.

Those who have had near-death experiences ay their entire life passes before them at that moment, but it seems that the dying one's life also passes before his loved ones as well, which is what we were experiencing as we sat beside his bed.

I've heard others say the soul will not move on until it knows that the loved ones are prepared and have given permission for the soul to move on. I believe at that moment, Clare, Dona, Mabel and myself granted Don that permission. His children were able to tell him what a good father he had been, a good provider for them and their mother, and a friend when they became adults–her "biggest cheerleader" as Dona once referred to him. They let him know it was OK to let go, and perhaps he heard and agreed.

The entire event was a strange mixture of nostalgia, mild horror, followed by an unexpected sense of peace–what one of our friends refers to as a 'strange grace.' I know we all felt that strange grace that afternoon in that cold hospital room in a tiny east Texas town, as we watched the end of a 92-year-long life that was very well lived.

PHOTOGRAPHIC MEMORY

(Originally Published in *Muscadine Lines: A Southern Journal*
October 2008.

She can't recall exactly when the Olan Mills man called, but my mother thinks it was probably early in the summer, since she was at home playing in the front yard. She can't recall his name, or much about what he looked like or what he drove, but even today, she still has trouble retelling the incident without the emotions washing over her afresh, reawakening the pain she first felt nearly three-quarters of a century ago.

My mother grew up in a two-story clapboard house on Danbury Avenue in Wellsville, Ohio, a tiny river town just to the north of Wheeling, West Virginia. A fire destroyed the house in 1936 and the family moved to another home a few blocks away on Chester Avenue.

Wellsville is barely three miles long and less than a mile wide, sandwiched between the Ohio River and the foothills of the Alleghenies. The twenty-five-block-long hamlet has ten churches, eleven bars, three grocery stores, two elementary schools and one high school. Just a few hundred yards to the west of the house on Danbury, the mountain rises quickly, a thousand feet or so, where it stands like a sentinel, guarding the peaceful hamlet from the storms that blow in from the flat corn country of central Ohio. The area was settled by British, Eastern European, and Italian immigrants drawn there by the plentiful work in the steel, coal and clay mining, and pottery industries.

When my mother was small, a constant stream of smoke from the nearby potteries, brickyards, and coal-fired power plants would drift across the town and downriver, sprinkling fly ash like fairy dust over the towns that lay to the south. At night, the whistles of the trains echoed off the mountain and sounded like they are coming through the bedroom walls. On Friday nights, the muted sounds of drums from the high school band, punctuated by intermittent bursts of cheering crowds, drifted from the football stadium at the lower end of town to my open bedroom window.

My grandfather, George Ernest Culp, was a railroad man, one of the fortunate few in the town who were able to work regularly during most of the Depression. Unfortunately, much of his paycheck never made it to the dinner table. The money often lost its way at the cashier window at Waterford Park racetrack or what was left of it was flushed down the urinal at the West End Tavern or at the Busy Bee Lounge.

I have only a few recollections of my grandfather, and they are vague and fading, since he died when I was just 10. I remember him sitting at his kitchen table with his two ever-present accouterments: his bean bag ashtray with the copper bottom, overflowing with filterless Camel cigarette butts, and the radio tuned to KDKA-AM out of Pittsburgh, "bringing you the best of Pirates baseball." Nature had given Grandpa a large nose to begin with, and it had become even more elongated, red, and bulbous from the overuse of his beverage of choice: red wine. During his retirement, he would seldom leave the kitchen table. Day after day, he would sit there, playing solitaire, listening to the radio, smoking, and grunting.

My grandmother, Margaret Ruth Culp, did her best to raise six children on what was left of my grandfather's paycheck each week. When he went through a sober spell, though, they managed to get by, and on rare occasions, there might even be a little left over. This may have been one of those rare occasions the day the photographer came to call, and he was intent on getting the surplus.

As my mother recalls, he drove up to the house, got out of his car and knocked on the front door, doffing his hat when my grandmother opened the screen door. He took a small bow, and introduced himself.

"I couldn't help but notice, Mrs. Culp, that you have toys in your yard. That couldn't mean that you have little ones running around here, could it?" he smiled obsequiously.

"Yes. This is my daughter, Jane..." Grandma said somewhat suspiciously from inside the front door, as my mother peered out from behind her legs "... and she's got five brothers and sisters, but most of them are older."

"Well, isn't she a cutie?" he said. "You know Mrs. Culp, these years really are the most precious, wouldn't you agree?"

"I suppose so," Grandma responded, still a little leery of the stranger.

"And wouldn't it be a travesty if we had nothing to remember those years by, Mrs. Culp?"

"What do you mean?" she asked.

"Well, the most precious gifts we can give our children are memories. And we at Olan Mills would like to help you. And right now we're offering a *free* photo just for taking the time to look at our products. Now if you let me show you some of our packages…" he said as he leaned toward the door.

"I really don't think we're interested," my grandmother said as she started to close the door.

"But we really do have some *very* reasonable packages," he insisted. "If you can just give me five more minutes of your time, I think you'll see what a great bargain this is." My grandmother just stared at him. "They're only young once," he said.

"OK. Five minutes," she conceded as she let him in the door.

"I don't think you'll regret it, Mrs. Culp."

The man continued talking as he entered the house. "You know, Mrs. Culp, in the three short years since Olan and Mary Mills started this company in a tiny office down in Chattanooga, Tennessee, we have become one of the fastest growing portrait companies in the country. And do you know why?" he asked, pulling out his paperwork from his briefcase. "It's because we offer *quality*. And that's what Americans appreciate, Mrs. Culp. *Quality*. We have quality products and quality people working for us. Now our basic packages start at...."

He laid out his samples and turned on the charm. He informed her that he had his camera in the car and would be happy to set it up take a nice photo of little Jane if she were so inclined. After a few moments of gentle coercion, my grandmother relented, and the man went to his car.

As he set up his equipment, my grandmother took my mother upstairs and put on her best Sunday dress. She trembled with anticipation as they descended the stairs and the photographer sat her atop the old upright piano in their living room, her hair now curled, a little rouge on her cheek. She waited patiently for the photographer to finish setting up his equipment. The flash bulbs popped several times and the man packed up his equipment, handed her his business card, and left with a polite "thank you."

The neighborhood kids often picked on my mother when she was small, as did her own brothers and sisters, for any number of reasons: her "go-funny" eye, her large teeth, her frizzy hair, or the way she mispronounced words. But that morning, for once, she felt special and pretty.

A few days later, my grandfather came home from a long trip on the railroad and informed his wife that she wasn't wasting any of his money on silly photographs. My grandmother gently broke the news to my mother.

When the photographer returned a week or so later, he tried the hard sell. He spread the black and white proofs on the table as my mother looked on, wondering which one she would get to keep. Remembering what her husband had told her, she tried her best to decline the offers and still retain her dignity.

"I don't think…" she said "I mean, we don't have a lot of money in our budget right now for pictures. But I thank you for your time, and I would like to take advantage of the free photo that you offered."

"Pardon me?" the man asked, now a little miffed.

"You know. You said last week we'd get one free photo just for our time," she persisted.

"Mrs. Culp," he replied sternly, "You get the free photo *after* you buy a package. It says so very clearly right here." He continued to press her, but to no avail. Finally, he said, "Now am I to understand that you are not going to purchase *any* of our fine products?"

"No, I'm afraid we just can't…"

Before she could finish, the salesman reached over to the stack of beautiful black and white photos lying on the kitchen table. My mother was standing next to the table. She could see herself in the fold of the proofs. She could see herself smiling ear to ear in her Sunday dress and dark black curls, atop the piano. It was the first time anyone had taken a picture of her. While my grandmother was still talking, the man said curtly, "Fine!"

It must have seemed as though he were moving in slow motion as my mother saw the 8" X 10" glossies being ripped, first in half, then in quarters, and finally in eighths before the man threw the tattered remnants back into his bag with a smirk and said, "Good day, madam."

My mother and grandmother watched him walk out of the house, down the front steps, and get in his car. The image of him driving away began to blur as her eyes moistened.

They stood at the door for a long time after he was gone. They said nothing to each other as he faded from view, but the words he uttered earlier still burned in their ears: *Quality, Mrs. Culp. Quality.*

CLAY

*"And the Lord God formed the man out of the clay
of the ground and breathed into his nostrils the
breath of life, and the man became a living being."*

GENESIS 2:7

Clay haunts me.

It seems to follow me everywhere I go. I walk into a restaurant in Glacier National Park, Montana, and it is there. In a cafe in Ixtapa, Mexico, it is there. In a hotel lobby in Baltimore, it is there. All I need to do to be reminded of the strained relationship I had with my father is to pick up a cup or saucer and turn it over. His lifeblood and mine are in the pottery that boasts the name of our hometown. The restaurant ware is a reminder to me of the clay that is mined from the hills of my hometown; it is also a reminder of my past that I can never entirely escape, and a reminder to me that one day, I shall return to that same clay rich soil.

I grew up in the area known as the Pottery Capitol of the World, the area of southeastern Ohio that borders the thin strip of the West Virginia Panhandle. Forty miles to the east is Pittsburgh, and the steel mill country of western Pennsylvania; to the west, the flat corn and wheat fields of central Ohio. The British, Italian, and Eastern European immigrants who settled in the area were drawn there by the two major industries—pottery and steel—which were the economic backbone of the area for nearly a century and a half.

It is a land that sits at a crossroads of cultures. It is a land where the corn and hog farmers outside of Wellsville, my hometown, make fun of the "river rats" in the small towns along Ohio, and the river rats do likewise.

Across the Ohio River, in West Virginia, a barely detectable southern accent emerges in the speech of the panhandlers. The accent becomes more pronounced the further one travels south, so that by the time you reach the Marietta/Parkersburg area, it is a full-fledged drawl. The Ohio folks consider themselves more sophisticated than those who live "down hoopie," as they call it, a reference to the poor mountain culture of West Virginia.

The people from my hometown are an interesting mix of cosmopolitan and redneck. It's where North meets South, politically and ideologically, as evidenced by the fact that the state voted for Al Gore in 2000, but went for George Bush in 2004, and Barak Obama in 2008. It is a true swing state.

This clash of cultures is sometimes reflected in the tense rivalries between Pittsburgh Steeler fans and Cleveland Brown fans; and between WVU Mountaineer fans and Ohio State Buckeye fans. The music of the area also reflects the paradox. It is the home of The Wheeling Jamboree, once the second most popular live country music radio show behind Nashville's Grand Ole Opry, and also the home of the 1980s funk band Wild Cherry ("Play That Funky Music White Boy") and other disco bands. Nearby Cleveland is home to the Rock 'n Roll Hall of Fame, and the area is proud of its rich musical heritage, from Chrissie Hynde of the Pretenders to Joe Walsh to the 1980s techno-pop band Devo.

When the British artisans settled here in the mid-19th century, they brought to the area their skill in designing pottery. The industry flourished because of the abundance of rich clay deposits in the hills. The town that lies two miles to the north of Wellsville is East Liverpool, which takes its name from the Mother Country, although no one really knows why it is not West Liverpool instead.

Men like my father drew the soft, wet, clay out of the ground and loaded it onto trucks that transported it to the area's brickyards and potteries. For generations, the area produced the restaurant ware—dinner plates, coffee cups, and saucers—for thousands of restaurants across much of North America. Skilled craftsmen etched designs onto the finer, high-end products that were sold to places like the Franklin Mint and today are traded among collectors. The most popular product in recent years has been the brightly colored line of Fiesta Ware that the Homer Laughlin plant produces.

The clay is poured into molds and the finished plates are fired in tall brick kilns, glazed, and put onto large crates before being shipped out. Each summer, the annual Pottery Festival, complete with a Pottery Queen, pays homage to the industry that prospered the area.

During the 1990s, however, the potteries began losing market share to imports, and began laying off workers. The Sterling China plant in Wellsville recently closed its doors, and the Homer Laughlin plant is barely hanging on. As for the clay mines and brickyards, they have nearly all been closed and boarded up.

My father spent much of his working life at the Pleasant Valley clay mine on State Route 45 just north of Wellsville. The PV mine sits on a sharp curve in the two-lane highway that gradually winds from town into a tiny community called Hillcrest. The mine was owned by the H.K. Porter Co, which also owned a brickyard at the south end of town. When he wasn't working at the clay mine, dad often worked at H.K. Porter, "hacking brick"—taking the hot bricks straight from the kilns and inspecting them for cracks before placing them on pallets. The arthritis he endured for many years was similar to carpal tunnel syndrome, and doubtless was a result of his time hacking brick. But back then, men didn't complain about such things. They just kept hacking until their arms fell off or they died. The final job he ever had, when he was in his 60s, was as a night watchman at the brickyard just before it shut down.

I was eight or nine years old when I went into the mines with my father for the first time. My best friend, Gregory Spann, and I were playing in my backyard.

As we played, I heard my father calling my name from the front yard. "Hey, Moochie, what 'ya doing?" my dad yelled. He had given me the nickname from a character in a Walt Disney movie.

"Nothing," I said. "Why?"

"Wanna take a ride out to PV with me?" he asked.

"Sure. Can Gregory come, too?" I asked.

"I don't care. Just tell him to call his mom and let her know," he said as he strolled toward the car, whistling and flipping a 50-cent piece that he had nearly worn the head off.

I was excited, but the mines still scared me. Clay was not combustible, so they didn't have the kind of explosions that the deep coal mines in West Virginia had, but they could still cave in, and sometimes did. My mild case of claustrophobia made the prospect daunting, but my desire to connect with my father was stronger than my fears, so I steeled my nerves and went.

Gregory and I hopped in the back seat of my dad's big, brown '65 Chevy with the 357 engine. A puff of clay dust rose from the seat as we sat down.

When we got to the mine, my dad gave us helmets with lights on them. We got into one of the cars, and began our descent. Water dripped from the walls of the mine as the car rumbled lower and lower. As we rode along, my dad told us how they extracted the clay from the walls of the mine and loaded it onto conveyor belts, which carried the clay to the trucks waiting above ground, where it was then transported to the local potteries and brickyards. We spend about an hour in the damp and dark ground before we hopped back in the car and made our ascent. My father told me they kept mapping this particular vein, but had never found the end of it yet.

When we went to school the next day, we couldn't wait to share our adventure with our friends. None of the other kids had ever been inside a mine before. It was one of the few occasions that I was able to get a glimpse into my father's life at work.

> *"Shall the clay say of the potter that made it, 'He hath made me not?' Or shall the thing framed say of him that framed it, 'He hath no understanding?'"*

ISAIAH 29:16

My father was raised in Toronto, Ohio, just a few miles down the river from Wellsville. He was the last of nine children. He never talked much about his childhood. One of the few things I knew about my paternal grandfather was that he often beat my father and his brothers and sisters if they dared to sneak a piece of bologna from his lunchbox. Dad told us later, this was the reason he swore never to beat his own children, especially for something like being hungry. And except for a few well-deserved swats on the bottom when we were small, he kept his word.

He worked the 3:00 to 11:00 shift when I was growing up, so he missed out on many of our childhood activities although he would occasionally materialize in the middle of a Friday night football game at the local high school stadium when we were playing, and then sneak back out just as quickly. I often wondered how he was able to talk his supervisors into letting him off for a couple of hours in the middle of a shift. My brother and I were both second stringers in high school, so he seldom got to see us actually play, but we always appreciated his efforts to be there.

Outside of those few occasions in the mines, the only significant time I spent with him was playing golf at the Par 3 Golf Course near Beaver Creek outside of East Liverpool. When I was in the sixth grade and my brother in the ninth, we began playing golf, and we picked it up pretty quickly. Soon after, my father took up the game as well. As a young man, he had been a good sandlot baseball player, and once hitchhiked to Cleveland to attend an open tryout for the Cleveland Indians. As a result, he had a natural swing that transferred to golf quite well, although he never really learned the rules or cared much about the etiquette.

It seemed like a strange hobby for a man who had spent most of his life working in mines. He never took a single lesson. On the Par 3 course, he used the same club—a 3 iron—nearly the whole round, sometimes even to putt. He never used a golf bag. He just stuck a couple of balls in his shirt pocket with his pack of cigarettes and off he'd go.

Despite the fact that I had been playing for three or four years when he picked up the game, I usually had to struggle to hold my own with him. He liked going to the course at 6:00 a.m. on Sunday mornings, before anyone else was there. He would come and roust me from a deep sleep and we would head out the door with some steaming coffee and hot tea. We would drive through the fog, silently, to the course and tee off from the wet grass just as the fog was rising from the fairways.

I now realize there was probably nothing about the sport itself that compelled him to play. I think it was his attempt to connect with me, the youngest of his three children, when he realized there would soon be an empty nest at his house. By this time, my sister Sherry had already moved to Washington, D.C. and my brother was preparing to go to Kent State. I think he realized that I would be gone soon, too and this was the only way he knew to reach out.

I only wish I saw it then. Too often, I just viewed those 6:00 a.m. Sunday morning wake-ups as an intrusion on my sleep. The season we shared on the golf course together was as precious and short-lived as the conversations we had as we strode through the course, side by side, the freshly cut grass sticking to our dew-soaked shoes, as the sun rose over Beaver Creek. It was one of only a few times I ever felt close to him.

My father drank when he was still single, but my mother, who had grown up with an alcoholic father, made him quit when they married. To my knowledge, he seldom touched it for the next thirty years, until after I went off to college. But the empty nest syndrome must have hit him then, and he began drinking again. He made up for lost time. Their marriage deteriorated quickly when I left for college and they separated.

About that time, our next-door neighbor passed away. My dad had always cared for Mr. Woomer and his wife in their latter years, taking them to the doctor and to the store for groceries and to pick up prescriptions. As a result, Mr. Woomer left my father his house in his will, so my father moved in. For the next 20 years, he and my mother lived next door to each other, still married, but rarely speaking.

After I graduated from college, the 30 percent unemployment rate in the area forced me to move to Tennessee to find work. For several years, when I made the trek back to Ohio to visit my family, it was rare to find my dad sober. I would sometimes get treated to stories from the townspeople about his escapades, which were becoming legendary in their minds. I really didn't want to know.

When I got married in 1998, my father didn't come to the wedding in Tennessee. I don't know which was sadder: the fact that he wasn't there, or the fact that I was almost relieved when I found out. His awkwardness in social situations, especially those in which he felt—erroneously, of course—that people were judging him, forced him to adopt the pre-emptive strike approach. He sometimes lashed out at others, ridiculing them as a result of his own insecurities. Had he come, I would have been on edge the entire weekend, afraid he might drink too much or say something to offend someone, and I probably couldn't have enjoyed my own wedding. The saddest thing is that, when he was sober, he was mostly enjoyable to talk to. He was knowledgeable in a lot of areas like politics and local history, and people never judged him the way he thought they did. But he always had his protective shields up when he was drinking.

During this dark season in his life, I went back home for Christmas one year and went to look for him. I found him at the Busy Bee Lounge, glassy-eyed and staggering. After I sat and tried to make conversation for a few minutes, one of his buddies asked him who I was. When my dad told him, his friend responded, "Hell, Rudder, I didn't know you had any kids!"

As I sat there, I thought back to my childhood, to a time when this same man would take me with him to visit Robert Nile, a shut-in in our neighborhood who had lost the use of his legs due to polio. As Robert sat there on the edge of his bed, with his blanket draped over his shoulders, telling us stories, my father listen for a while, but would eventually get antsy and leave. He always instructed me to stay and visit with Robert, though. My father was also known to stop by a neighbor's house and take one or more of their small children by the hand to the neighborhood grocery store for an ice cream sandwich, just to give their mothers a break. He often gave what little extra money he had to other neighbors who were down on their luck, and of course, always to me when I was at college or as a young man. Those were the glimpses I got to see of his compassionate side, so I didn't judge him too harshly now.

That night, at the Busy Bee, I sat at the bar, watching the Indian paddling his canoe across the electronic Hamm's beer sign, and listening to Alan Jackson on the jukebox, before I finally snuck out the door. I'm not sure he even noticed.

As I left, the thick snowflakes began to fall harder over the shops on Main Street. I could hear carols chiming from the manger scene at the First Christian Church, mingled with loud voices still cursing inside the Busy Bee. I walked down Riverside Avenue, where many of the old historic homes were in severe need of repair. As a result of the economic downturn following the collapse of the local steel and pottery industries, the idyllic Bedford Falls-like hometown where I had grown up had morphed into "Pottersville." My tears blurred the light from the lampposts as I began to walk through town. I wondered how many of my friends had spent their Christmas Eve trying to track down their fathers in a bar.

I watched the chunks of ice floating in the Ohio River and eventually crossed back over Main Street to Commerce, where I passed by the empty Sterling China plant. The silent, vacant factory buildings and the dilapidated, boarded up homes in the dying industrial town made me think of death.

> *"When he had said these things, He spat on the ground and made clay with the saliva, and he anointed the eyes of the blind man with the clay."*

JOHN 9:6

I was on my way to a concert by the Irish duo, Keith and Kristyn Getty, on the evening of December 18, 2009 when I got the call. My wife and I were in the car with my daughter Abigail when my cell phone began vibrating. It was my mother. She tried her best to soften the blow, but I knew instinctively, like many children know, why she was calling before she even spoke. It was the call that every son or daughter dreads.

She told me no one in the family had seen or heard from my dad for several days. When my brother went to check on him that Sunday afternoon, he found him dead in his apartment. The coroner said he had been there two, maybe three days.

We buried him two days before Christmas. There were nearly three feet of snow on the ground.

Earlier in my life, I often thought about this day and what it would be like, and how I would respond. The day when he would be laid back into the clay-rich soil that he mined for much of his life. I often worried that, when he was gone, I might regret that I hadn't tried harder to connect with him while he was here.

And I was right.

My father was sober the last three or four years of his life and seemed more like the dad I had known growing up: more approachable, but still not exactly warm. We talked on the phone a few times, although the conversations were typically shorter than five minutes. Now I try to view his life in its entirety, particularly the early and late years. It is from the perspective of these bookends that I choose to remember him, rather than the lost decades in the middle.

These days, I seldom see the dinner plates that read "Sterling China, Wellsville, Ohio" or "Homer Laughlin China," on the bottom. But when I do, I am back on Main Street at

Christmas time. Or sitting next to my father on the edge of Robert Nile's bed. Or walking beside him in the dewy grass at the Beaver Creek Par 3 golf course as the sun begins to peek through the fog. Or riding beside him in a mining cart at the Pleasant Valley Mine on a cold November day, desperate to reach out and take his hand in mine, as we descend into the earth together.

Notes

1. W.H. Auden, *"Musée des Beaux Arts,"* *Collected Poems*, E. Mendelson, Ed. Vintage Reprint edition, 2007.

2. Lyle Crist, "Take the Stars with You" from *Afterwords: An English Prof's Reflections on a Campus Career.* Copyright by Lyle Crist. Published by Mount Union College, 1989.

3. Susanna Clark, Jim Janosky, Guy Clark. "The Cape," Copyright: Susanna Clark Music/Comet Music/Sony/ATV Music Publishing LLC.

4. Mark Victor Hansen, Jack Canfield, and Randy Rudder. *Chicken Soup for the Soul: Country Music Edition.* Chicken Soup for the Soul Books, 2011.

5. James Wright, "Autumn Begins in Martin's Ferry, Ohio," *The Branch Will Not Break*, Wesleyan University Press, Copyright 1959, 1960, 1961, 1962, 1963.

6. Wayne Dyer, *Wishes Fulfilled: Mastering the Art of Manifesting.* Hay House Publishing, 2012.

7. Annie Proulx, Introduction to *A River Runs Through It and Other Stories: Twenty-fifth Anniversary Edition.* University of Chicago Press, 2009

8. Truman Capote, *In Cold Blood.* Vintage International Edition, Random House, 2001.

9. Emily Dickinson, "This Quiet Dust Was Gentlemen and Ladies." *Poems.* Nabu Press, 2010.

Made in United States
Cleveland, OH
01 March 2025